ELITE WRESTLING

MOVES FOR SUCCESS ON AND BEYOND THE MAT

TOM RYAN

WITH JULIE SAMPSON
PHOTOGRAPHY BY BRUCE CURTIS

Published by Echo Point Books & Media
Brattleboro, Vermont
www.EchoPointBooks.com

All rights reserved.
Neither this work nor any portions thereof may be reproduced, stored in a retrieval system, or transmitted in any capacity without written permission from the publisher.

Copyright © 2007, 2017 by Julie Sampson, Bruce Curtis & Thomas Ryan

Elite Wrestling
ISBN: 978-1-62654-604-2

Photography by Bruce Curtis

Cover design by Adrienne Núñez
Cover photograph: "Mango Lifts Tellgren,"
U.S. Army photo by Tim Hipps, FMWRC Public Affairs

This book is dedicated in loving memory of Teague William Ryan. The inspiration for this book, Teague was the mascot for the Hofstra University wrestling team during the 2003–2004 season. He died tragically on February 16, 2004.

Contents

	Acknowledgments	ix
	Introduction: The Will to Wrestle	xi
1	**Wrestling Is a Marathon, Not a Sprint** *Coach Tom Ryan, Ohio State University*	1
2	**In Defense of Wrestling** *Donald Rumsfeld, U.S. Secretary of Defense*	9
3	**Whatever, Whoever, Whenever Wrestling** *Dan Gable, Legendary Coach and Wrestler*	15
4	**No Elbows, No Knees, No Excuses** *Kyle Maynard, Author and Motivational Speaker*	23
5	**The Code of Coaching Ethics** *Coach Terry Brands, U.S. Olympic Freestyle Wrestling*	31
6	**Making the Grade** *Coach Jay Weiss, Harvard University; Coach Brendan Buckley, Columbia University*	37
7	**As Good as It Gets** *Stephen Neal, New England Patriots*	43
8	**Promoting Your Program** *Coach J Robinson, University of Minnesota*	49
9	**Speaking of Wrestling** *Dennis Hastert, Speaker of the U.S. House of Representatives*	55

Contents

10 Pioneer in Women's Wrestling — 61
Tricia Saunders, World Champion Wrestler

11 Role of the Assistant Coach — 67
Assistant Coach Jim Heffernan, University of Illinois; Assistant Coaches Donny Pritzlaff and Rob Anspach, Hofstra University

12 Surrounding Yourself with Good People — 75
Ben Peterson, Olympic Gold Medalist

13 Peaking Throughout the Season and the Essence of Speed — 81
Coach Carl Adams, Boston University

14 Wrestling Leads to Nobel Peace Prize — 89
Dr. Norman Borlaug, 1970 Nobel Peace Prize Winner

15 Learning from Losing — 95
Coach Tom Brands, University of Iowa

16 Running a Tournament — 99
Ken Kraft, Father of the Midlands Tournament

17 A Call to Serve Others — 105
Father John McLaughlin

18 The Will to Overcome Tragedy — 111
Timothy Donovan

19 The Year-Round Wrestler — 117
Jim Zalesky, Former University of Iowa Coach and Wrestler

20 Building Team Unity — 121
Coach Greg Strobel, Lehigh University; Coach T. J. Kerr, California State University, Bakersfield; and Coach Tom Borrelli, Central Michigan University

21 Making the Right Call — 131
Dr. Vincent Zuaro, Referee

Contents

22	**The Edge of Mental Toughness** *Coach Steve Fraser, U.S. Olympic Greco-Roman Wrestling*	135
23	**Seize the Moment** *Sam Kline, All-American at West Virginia University*	141
24	**The Role of Supportive Parents** *Advice from Fathers in the Coaching Corner*	147
25	**My Two Champions** *John Irving, Writer and Former Prep School Coach*	159
26	**Wrestling with Politics** *James Jordan, Ohio Senator*	165
27	**He Stands Alone** *Coach Jack Spates, University of Oklahoma*	169
28	**Drills**	171

    Knock-Out Drill   172
    Down Block Drill   174
    High Crotch Head Block Spin Drill   176
    Squaring Hips Drill   178
    Single Leg Head Block Spin Drill   180
    Monkey Grip Go Behind Drill   182
    Snap a Wrist to an Underhook Throw-By Drill   186
    Post Triceps Drill   190
    Knee Slide Drill   193
    Bull Fight Drill   195
    Hip Heist Drill   199
    Stand-Up Mat Return Drill   201
    Spiral Ride Claw Drill   203

Index   205

Acknowledgments

Tom Ryan
- Teague William Ryan, for the gift of five incredible years, and for your ever-present spirit that helps me to better understand the connection between the spiritual world and what my purpose is in this world.
- Lynette, Jordan, Jake, and Mackenzie—thank you for your endless love and support.
- My parents, for a loving, secure, positive environment and for all of your encouragement that helps me to follow my dream.
- My brother Frank, for your endless love and support and for being a great role model. The journey through life has been made better with you alongside me.
- My sister Kim, your intense spirit and love have graced my life.
- Alumni and friends of Hofstra wrestling who have generously supported me in the best of times and the worst of times.
- Julie Sampson, for your vision, drive, and tireless work ethic that went into creating this book.
- Coaches, teammates, and friends who challenged me to be a better person.
- Parents of student-athletes and the student-athletes who have selected Ohio State University, for allowing me to be a part of your lives.

Julie Sampson
- John, my voice of reason, "Nothing worthwhile is ever easy."
- Troy and Sheila Mae, my reason for being. "That's what I'm talking about!"
- Sheila Griffin, your Irish eyes are always smiling in my mind.
- My parents, for always being there.
- Tom Ryan, thanks for teaching me about wrestling and life.
- Chaminade Coach George Dlugolonski, for inspiring generations of wrestlers.

A special note of appreciation for all those people who helped to make this book possible: McGraw-Hill Professional senior editor

Acknowledgments

Mark Weinstein, senior project editor Jenn Tust, and literary agent Rita Rosenkrantz. Also, Jack Magnani and Mike Torriero for the drills.

A special overall thanks to the following people for taking the time to be interviewed and for generously lending their expertise to this book: Dennis Hastert, U.S. Speaker of the House of Representatives; Donald Rumsfeld, U.S. secretary of defense; Dan Gable, Ken Kraft, Dr. Norman Borlaug, Kyle Maynard, Ben Peterson, Carl Adams, Terry Brands, Tom Brands, Jack Childs, Terrence Kerr, J Robinson, John Irving, Jack Spates, Greg Strobel, Jim Heffernan, Tom Borrelli, Steve Fraser, Stephen Neal, The New England Patriots, Jim Zalesky, Fr. John McLaughlin, Tim Donovan, Dr. Vincent Zuaro, Jay Weiss, Brendan Buckley, Gary Abbott, Tricia Saunders, Rob Anspach, Donny Pritzlaff, Jesse Jantzen, Don Jantzen, Steven Churella, Al Bevilacqua, Ryan Bonfiglio, Sam Kline, and Jim Jordan.

Introduction: The Will to Wrestle

So, what is it about wrestlers?

Some people are born competitors. There is nothing that can stop them. They move through life actually generating more energy and drive to overcome the same boundaries that stop virtually everybody else. The sport of wrestling was custom designed for this breed of person.

The life lessons that are learned on the wrestling mat never diminish; in fact, most wrestlers carry that same focus, discipline, and drive into their professional lives. When the life skills that are learned in wrestling translate into the real world, here's what happens:

- You can be like Donald Rumsfeld, the U.S. secretary of defense.
- You can be like Dennis Hastert, the U.S. Speaker of the House of Representatives.
- You can be like Dr. Norman Bourlag, the 1970 Nobel Peace Prize recipient.
- You can be like Kyle Maynard, a wrestler born with congenital amputation who learned to wrestle and be a winner in the game of life.
- You can be like John Irving, a famous American writer.
- You can be like Stephen Neal, an offensive guard for the three-time Super Bowl Champion New England Patriots.
- You can be like Dan Gable, the legendary wrestler and coach.
- You can be like Tricia Saunders, a pioneer in women's wrestling.

You can be anything you set your mind to because wrestling prepares you for life.

It is a gift to train and compete in wrestling. For those fortunate people who realize that their gifts can help shape future generations of wrestlers, they are proud to be coaching wrestling.

Today's wrestling coach is a multifaceted creature: one of great leadership, patience, discipline, compassion, knowledge, and focus.

Introduction

Think of the hours of instruction in physical conditioning, technique training, and drilling. A wrestling coach has to have a high level of patience in offering guidance with technique and nutritional advice to determined athletes. He has to know what to say to help celebrate the thrill of a victory or to help understand the pain of a loss. There is no easy road to coaching a wrestling team and no known secret success formula, but there are some top coaches in the country willing to share their perspectives on how they try to shape what is the oldest sport known to mankind.

The pages that follow are a showcase of heartfelt experiences in competition, coaching, and life from amazing people who are who they are because of their association with wrestling.

So, what is it about wrestlers?

Read on.

1
Wrestling Is a Marathon, Not a Sprint

Coach Tom Ryan, Ohio State University

I have learned a lot about life through my experiences with wrestling, both as a wrestler and as a coach. The testimonies from other wrestlers about what the sport has meant in their lives always fascinates me. Everyone seems to have a story.

If you think for a moment about the circle in the center of a wrestling mat, it seems to represent life; there is no clear beginning and there is no clear ending. In the middle of that circle is one human working his strategy, strength, and technique against another. On many days, the battle

in the circle reflects the wrestler who has outworked the other. Sometimes the gift of athleticism prevails over hard work. Other times, it comes down to a judgment call or the clock running out of time. Occasionally, luck becomes a factor, good luck for one, and bad luck for another.

Inside that circle lessons are learned that do not end with wins and losses. Many wrestlers who reflect on their time spent in wrestling find that the things that took place on the mat are what have driven them through life.

In this chapter, I share my insights on coaching and what I am trying to pass on to the next generation of wrestlers who are learning to face the challenges inside the circle of life. I don't claim to have all the answers, which is why this book features interviews with a wide variety of wrestlers who are all intriguing in their own way.

For Tom Ryan, head wrestling coach at Ohio State University, winning certainly is a sweet reward from lots of year-round hard work, but it is not even close to being the main focus of his program. In Ryan's eyes, the key to his success as a coach is when he inspires his athletes to reach a personal epiphany—when they discover their higher purpose in life.

"My job as a coach is to motivate my wrestlers. The last thing I want to do is judge them. All I can ask of them is to give some thought to why they are here on Earth. We are not put here by accident, so why are we here?" Ryan has asked.

That question alone is more challenging than any practice session or collegiate wrestling match. *Why are we here?*

It wasn't always this way with Ryan. After 14 years of coaching and a lifetime of competing in wrestling, there was a time when training, making weight, and, of course, the competition itself was his prime directive in life. Eventually, Ryan's focus shifted to finding a deeper understanding of what wrestling is all about.

"That is the way it is for many people involved in wrestling, which is good to a point, but there is so much more to it than that. There is something far greater than winning championships. My goal is to help my wrestlers figure out what that is," he said.

It took something far beyond the depths of wrestling to open Ryan's eyes to the meaning of life, leading to his personal epiphany.

Ryan was in the midst of a successful wrestling season in February 2004. He was at his Long Island home in Hauppauge, New York,

Tom Ryan works his opponent from the top as a wrestler for Coach Dan Gable's Iowa Hawkeyes. Ryan took second place in the NCAA finals at 158 pounds in 1991 and finished third in 1992.
(Photo courtesy of the University of Iowa Sports Information Department.)

with his wife, Lynette, and four children, Jordan, Jake, Teague, and Mackenzie. The Ryan family had just finished dinner when Teague, the Ryan's five-year-old son, suddenly stopped breathing. Ryan tried to revive his son with CPR, but Teague died tragically in his father's arms. As it was later determined, a rare disorder of the heart's electrical rhythm claimed Teague's life.

"I think about Teague all the time. Where is he? What was the purpose of his death? Where will I find the strength to carry on for the rest of our family? I have to believe that Teague's death will make me a better person. I have to believe there is a higher calling and a plan," Ryan shared.

Ryan had a tight bond with Teague as he had spent an enormous amount of time with him every day of his life. Teague was the mascot of the Hofstra wrestling team. Loved by the whole team, he spent a large part of his life in the Hofstra wrestling room.

"I always told my wrestlers that once you've wrestled, everything else in life is easy. I can't even come close to saying that anymore," Ryan said.

Teague Ryan, 5, sits next to his father, Coach Tom Ryan, on the Hofstra University bench. The team mascot in the 2004 season, Teague died tragically in February of that season. (Photo courtesy of Bruce Curtis.)

So what is it that helped Ryan carry on after suffering such an enormous loss? Perhaps he has figured out that the purpose in life is to get to heaven and that when he gets there, Teague will be waiting for him with open arms. Ryan moves carefully through each day, with some days being more difficult than other days, striving to be the best husband, the best father, the best coach, and the best person that he knows how to be.

In the days of coaching before the loss of his son, Ryan believes that he often put the individual wrestler first. Now, he realizes, the focus must be on the team as a whole and not on the individual. Wrestling is a team sport, and it should be coached that way.

Ryan establishes clear boundaries with solid team rules. The rules are reviewed at the start of each season, and each wrestler has to sign a contract showing that he agrees to them. Members of the coaching staff make sure that all of the rules are understood and adhered to with no exceptions. The team meets as a group regularly, coaches meet individually with the athletes, and through good communication everyone stays on track. A wrestler getting into trouble is not acceptable for any program. A coach must hold his wrestlers accountable for every little thing. Coaching is not a popularity contest. All problems must be addressed immediately and professionally, before the situation escalates.

"As a coach you cannot let one individual pollute the team. You have to set clear ultimatums. Unfortunately, sometimes things don't work out and you have to have an athlete say good-bye to wrestling. Basically, that individual has chosen not to do it. We all make our own choices and have to live with the outcome," he said.

Ryan believes that wrestling is just as much an internal battle as it is an external battle. Success needs to be measured not by winning percentages and records, but by simply asking yourself if you achieved what you were capable of achieving. If you can answer yes to that, then you had success. Each wrestler has to live up to his own potential. Sometimes you can win and not be satisfied with your performance, and sometimes you can lose, but feel pleased with your effort.

"It's a tough philosophy to follow, but it's not healthy to measure yourself with wins and losses. Society sets us up so that we think we have to achieve the highest and have the best of everything or else we're not satisfied. We have to get out of the habit of thinking that way. Your conscience will ultimately get to you. If you do everything that you are supposed to do, then you will have the success that you are capable of achieving. I really believe that. I think that the harder you work, the more confidence you build up, and those things really go hand in hand," he said.

When Ryan was a rookie coach out of college, he thought if you wrestled, then you naturally could coach the sport. But he learned soon that coaching and wrestling are completely different. As a coach you have to deal with people from all walks of life. As a wrestler, your main focus is yourself. A coach has to worry about so many details while keeping in mind all of the different personalities involved with the program. It takes time to mold a program using what you have available. It is crucial for a coach to know the level of his athletes, concentrate on the lesser strengths, and work on making improvements. And, Ryan believes that the coaching staff must take very seriously the fact that parents are entrusting you with their children.

"It is important to know your wrestlers as individuals. It is pretty easy to assess a person's athletic abilities, but it is a far greater chal-

lenge to really get to know a person and what makes them tick. Sometimes it can be surprising where you think you know a person and they do something that was unexpected. Some wrestlers can go through a program and deep down inside you question yourself if you fully reached them," Ryan said. "It's tough because there is no barometer to measure how much you got through to a person. Sometimes I wonder if not being able to fully reach a wrestler cost him in some way. I ask myself: What did I do to reach him? Did I do everything that I possibly could have? If I can answer those questions positively, then I can sleep at night."

The key to Ryan's coaching success is that what he demands from his wrestlers, he gives right back to them. He demands respect, and, in turn, he does not judge his athletes but looks for ways to help them improve. He offers constructive criticism and advice, and, in return, he expects steady improvements from his team. The team needs to see that its coach will do everything he can to help them reach their goals. As a coach it is especially crucial not to turn your back on a wrestler when he is struggling. A coach needs to be there for him when he is having success and when he is in a slump.

"As a coach I tell myself that as much as I love wrestling, my priorities have to be in place or else I will fall short. I ask myself and I challenge my team to get to know what their fundamental beliefs are. When you wake up in the morning, you have to ask yourself what your priorities are," he said.

Ryan stresses academics as a top priority. Once Ryan is certain academics are covered, he has a well-structured workout plan for his team and he expects steady weight control in order to avoid significant fluctuations in weight with each athlete.

"Nutrition and weight control are huge. We make sure everyone is on the same page with nutrition. It is so important to keep weight under control and not bounce up and down," Ryan said. "Each wrestler needs to find the right balance between his own nutrition and how it affects his weight. By keeping his weight steady, a wrestler can stay healthier and not get burned out in the middle of the season.

"Taking some time off is important, too. A coach has to carefully structure team workouts. For two days after a major competition, you should take it easy. You should definitely not overtrain in the weeks before a major competition. There are many people who think,

let's work like crazy in the weeks leading up to a major competition. I tend to ease up on the workouts at that time," he added.

Ryan displays a fine dichotomy between intensity and lightheartedness, and those are the elements that he brings to his wrestling room. He takes into consideration that wrestling is an intense sport, but he makes a conscious effort to keep it as fun as possible.

Although the emphasis today in youth sports is to specialize in one sport at an early age, Ryan believes very strongly that there is a real need for parents and children to still stay with the theory of the three-sport athlete. Playing a variety of sports helps with overall coordination and conditioning as well as maintaining a certain level of social benefits. In addition, participating in more than one sport allows for cross-training when it comes to footwork, balance, and cardiovascular conditioning.

"You need to create an environment where you succeed, but not be overbearing. The actual work itself is difficult enough; there's no need for me to be hard on everyone," he explained. "I like to make the pre-practice meetings fun. We share a lot at that time, too. Sometimes I read to the team if I find something they might be interested in. Sometimes the guys get together to play indoor soccer so that they have some laid-back time together and get to know each other as teammates. We have Christmas parties and beginning of the year parties. We do all sorts of things off the wrestling mat to promote team unity. This creates a level of trust. The team needs to know that I am behind them every step of the way. They need to know that when I say something, I mean it."

No matter what age or level of wrestler a coach is involved with, Ryan believes coaches need to remember that wrestling is a marathon and not a sprint. It is important to keep it fun for all wrestlers, because if a coach or the philosophy of a program turns away an athlete, he is probably lost from the sport forever.

2
In Defense of Wrestling

*Donald Rumsfeld,
U.S. Secretary of Defense*

If there is a relationship between effort and application equaling results, as Donald Rumsfeld, U.S. secretary of defense, says, then what better place to test this theory than on the wrestling mat?

That's just what Rumsfeld did when he wrestled for New Trier High School in Winnetka, Illinois, just north of Chicago. He got involved in wrestling mainly because he was too small for basketball. He soon found himself the captain of a state-championship-caliber team. His efforts were also applied in

the classroom, and by his senior year in 1950, he was offered scholarships to several Big 10 universities.

The Rumsfelds were a middle-class family. Rumsfeld's father, George, sold real estate but joined the Navy at the age of 38 shortly after World War II broke out, instilling in his son a lasting appreciation for government and military service as well as a deep sense of patriotism. The family moved frequently during the war before settling in suburban Chicago. Rumsfeld's parents were supportive of his wrestling efforts, and his father went to most of his matches. When it came time to look at colleges, the Rumsfelds encouraged their son to take an offer from a Big 10 school.

"The dean at my high school told me that I was not going to go to a Big 10 school—that I was going to go to Princeton instead. I told him that Princeton was too expensive. He told me he would help me get an academic scholarship so that I could go there. He was right. He pushed for me to go there, and, initially, it had never crossed my mind," Rumsfeld said.

He did go to Princeton, and while there, Rumsfeld continued to practice his theory that effort and application and results share a tight connection. He was undefeated his freshman year in wrestling. As a junior, he finished second at 157 pounds in the Eastern Intercollegiate Wrestling Association (EIWA). During his senior year, he captained the team, was undefeated in the regular season, and finished fourth in the Easterns. In one match against Cornell, Rumsfeld separated his shoulder, endured the pain, and went on to win the match by points.

"That's the nature of wrestling," he said. "It is a very tough sport. You are part of a team, but you are out there on your own. I originally went out for basketball in high school, but I was not tall and not particularly good. I went with a friend to a wrestling match, and I just took to it. It was serendipity that led me to wrestling, but it was the actual enjoyment of wrestling that kept me going."

That enjoyment lasted for 12 years before a shoulder injury kept him from pursuing Olympic hopes. After Princeton, Rumsfeld, like his father, served in the Navy. He was an aviator and flight instructor in the wake of the Korean War. He was also an All-Navy wrestling champion at 160 pounds in 1956.

"There's really not one single highlight that stands out in my mind from wrestling," Rumsfeld said. "I was at a big dinner in New York a

Donald Rumsfeld wrestled for Princeton and was an All-Navy wrestler.
(Photo courtesy of Office of Secretary of Defense Media Support.)

few years ago where I saw a lot of old friends and coaches and people I knew from wrestling going back 20 and 30 years. I hadn't seen these people in years. I was asked to speak and when I looked out at the crowd and all the faces from wrestling from over the years I just said, 'I love wrestling!' I really feel that way. It has been such an important part of my life."

After his years in active duty, Rumsfeld worked as an aide on Capitol Hill and later as an investment broker. In 1962, at the age of 30, he won a House of Representatives seat from an Illinois district, and he retained that seat in Congress for three subsequent elections.

In 1969 he resigned his House seat to work in President Richard Nixon's White House, first as director of the Office of Economic Opportunity and ultimately as U.S. ambassador to NATO.

Rumsfeld first served as secretary of defense under President Gerald Ford from 1975 to 1977 before resuming the position in 2001 under President George W. Bush. In 1977 Rumsfeld was awarded the Presidential Medal of Freedom, the nation's highest civilian award. When Ford picked Rumsfeld to be the 13th secretary of defense in 1975, Rumsfeld was 43 years old. When he became the 21st defense secretary, under George W. Bush in January 2001, he was 69, making

him both the youngest and the oldest person to serve as secretary of defense. Rumsfeld has led the U.S. armed forces into two wars in the aftermath of September 11th. His name forever will be associated with managing the Department of Defense during some of the most perilous times this nation has faced. He has led military operations against the Taliban, beginning in late 2001, and then, starting in 2005, in the ongoing struggle in Iraq.

Although he is inundated with the demands of leading the United States, he enjoys taking some time to talk about the sport that has meant so much in his life.

"Perseverance is another thing learned by people who wrestle. You learn this by will and attitude. It takes discipline to be persistent," Rumsfeld said. "I played other sports, but wrestling was clearly the sport I grew to love. I loved the competition. Wrestling is so complicated. There is nothing simple about it. But it's like anything else in life. Once you discipline yourself, whether it's reading a certain amount of time every day or practicing a musical instrument, the more you see progress, the more you enjoy doing it."

In his younger days, Rumsfeld the wrestler was preemptive, preferring to initiate the first move so that his opponent had to react to him. One of his favorite moves was the fireman's carry, in which he would drop to one knee, shoot under his opponent's leg, and throw him over his shoulder before dumping him on the mat. The move requires quickness and strength, Rumsfeld's specialties.

Thinking about wrestling and where it fits into today's world, Rumsfeld would like to see more people just go out and try it. There are programs available in every state in America, and he would like to see young Americans take advantage of the opportunity to get involved in wrestling.

"My first advice to young people is to go out and try it. The wonderful advantage to wrestling is that size does not matter. There is a weight class available for you. Some sports require speed, height, and size. Wrestling is the perfect sport from that regard because there are no requirements," he explained.

Wrestling is a sport that attracts a wide variety of people, regardless of physical attributes, and it also does not discriminate based on race, creed, or economic status. Essentially, wrestling is a sport for everyone.

"I think that once you try wrestling and take to it, then it is important to seek out competition better than you are so that you challenge yourself. That is true in life. That's the advice I have given to my own children. I have told them to seek out the brightest people you can imagine so that you can be around them, meet them, and stimulate yourself. You need to get interested in a wide variety of things. If you are interested in wrestling, then you should go find the best wrestlers you can and become a student of the sport," Rumsfeld explained.

Having spent 12 years as a student of the sport, Rumsfeld has an appreciation for the dedication many coaches put forth to keep the wrestling tradition alive.

"There are some truly wonderful coaches around our country. I am not in a position to give advice to coaches, but a coach's biggest job is to get through the walls of distraction. A coach has to break through the sound barrier to keep people interested in the sport and stimulated by the sport. Everybody gets to a point where you don't want to do something anymore. It's so easy to drop out and not complete something. A coach has the ability to help youngsters in America overcome that," Rumsfeld said.

Many college wrestling programs have been dropped over the years due to the negative interpretation of Title IX. Even Princeton's 100-year-old wrestling program faced possible extinction, but former wrestlers rallied and raised the funds to maintain the rich tradition of the sport at the institution.

"There are some wonderful schools that do have wrestling. It enables a whole group of people to succeed at something," Rumsfeld said.

Rumsfeld's firsthand experiences with wrestling have made him an advocate for preserving the sport in the academic world.

"America needs variety. People should not be driven toward sports with the greatest revenue. There have been a number of sports dropped, among them wrestling. Thanks to some good folks at Princeton, it was sustained. I think it's important to provide enough opportunities for all people," Rumsfeld said. He added, "There is something about wrestling that is unlike other sports. It contributes to developing self-confidence that helps people in life. Once a person has experienced the nature of wrestling, they come away with self-confidence."

Rumsfeld knows he was fortunate to have discovered wrestling and that he had the opportunity to combine athletics with his academic aptitude. Interestingly, the same dean at New Trier High School who told Rumsfeld to go to Princeton also told him who he was going to take to the prom.

"The dean pulled me aside in the hallway and told me who I was going to take to the prom. He told me don't even think about taking someone else. So the dean set up my prom date with Joyce Pierson. Now I've been married to her for 51 years," he happily reported. The Rumsfelds have three children and five grandchildren.

While his theory that there is a relationship between effort and application equals results has been proven true, it's fortunate that Rumsfeld left a little room for serendipity in his life as well. If he hadn't, then he would have never discovered his love for wrestling—or Joyce Pierson.

3
Whatever, Whoever, Whenever Wrestling

Dan Gable, Legendary Coach and Wrestler

There's a popular poster that features the intense face of legendary coach and wrestler Dan Gable with his quote, "Once you've wrestled, everything else in life is easy."

When you talk to Gable, there are no hints of easiness about him. He is a man filled with passion, with one of his greatest passions, next to his family, being wrestling. He is so passionate about wrestling, about his days as a competitor and his days as a coach, that just driving through certain areas makes him nervous.

Dan Gable's success as a wrester and as a wrestling coach is legendary.
(Photo courtesy of the University of Iowa Sports Information Department.)

"It doesn't matter whatever, whoever, or wherever, some things make me nervous. I can drive back to the college town in Ames, Iowa, and I'll start looking around and I'm instantly ready to go. I go to Oklahoma and I get nervous. I think about wrestlers from Russia and Iran and that takes me up to a new level immediately. These feelings never go away. It's been a part of me from the beginning," Gable said.

In the beginning, there was Gable the young wrestler who had an amazing run through high school and college, compiling a combined 182-1 record. He won 117 matches at Iowa State, including two NCAA championships before he was upset in his senior year in the 1970 NCAA Final. Washington sophomore Larry Owings, who was normally a 150-pounder, cut weight to drop into Gable's 142-pound weight class because he wanted to challenge him. Gable tied the match 8–8 after he trailed 7–2, but Owings reached deep to pull off a 13–11 upset.

"I lost that match in college because I let that other guy get inside my head. I got word that he was out to get me. I was getting lots of ink in the press, and I started reading about how this guy was out to get me. I wasn't focused. I forced myself to learn from that experience. I took that negative and turned it into something positive. Once you make a commitment, then you have to keep making improvements. You always need to learn from the path or the route you're taking," Gable said.

Gable rebounded quickly, winning the gold medal in the 149-pound class at the 1972 Olympics in Munich. Gable pinned three opponents and never gave up a point in six Olympic matches. After the Olympics, he took over as head coach at the University of Iowa in 1976 where he led the Hawkeyes to 15 national titles in 21 seasons. His teams went undefeated seven times and won the Big 10 title 21 times under his direction. His career coaching record is 355-21-5.

Dan Gable discusses strategy with one of his Hawkeye wrestlers during a break in the match.
(Photo courtesy of the University of Iowa Sports Information Department.)

"I've been trying to be a champion athlete since grade school," Gable said. "I've spent my whole life trying to upgrade and promote the sport at the highest levels. I hope my legacy will continue after I'm gone."

Gable, 57, is not even close to being done. "The best is yet to come," he said. And there's no doubt it will come. "I want to continue to do things. There are more motivating pieces to this. I find the world of wrestling to be very rewarding. I keep going with this sport to stay current. It's like raising a family; you have to stay on top of it, even though you're not totally in control. There's always something happening."

Gable likes to compare the old-style approaches to the new ones, but he is quick to add that he sees value in both.

"You have to realize what's more important. Thirty years ago they would lock you in the wrestling room and turn the heat up high and not give you any water. The old philosophy was that if you were practicing and working hard, you would never stop for water. There was discipline in that. You were weak if you stopped to drink water. Now, science tells us that drinking water throughout a workout is important. So many people would get so tired. You have to stay hydrated. Now you look at those two extremes and weigh them. You have to work toward keeping with the updated science. You also have to learn to become accustomed to things. Thirty years ago if you got hurt and went down, that was a sign of weakness. You got right back up and continued to wrestle. Now, if you get hurt, you stop, put ice on the injury, and rest. Science tells us that is the better approach because you heal faster," he explained.

Gable sees a big difference between the current world of wrestlers and the world where he developed. "It is so easy to be spoiled today. People are not as tough as they used to be. If you need to cut a tree down, who would use an ax? You get a chain saw to cut the tree down, right? There are kids who can't use a shovel to clear snow from a sidewalk or mow the lawn without using a ride-on mower. We're accustomed to clicking buttons and using remotes for everything. If the power goes out what are we going to do?" Gable wondered. "I think we need more of a mix today so that toughness and strength can be developed. We can maintain some of the old philosophies and apply them to today's rules."

Coach Dan Gable had his share of successes, but his main focus as a coach was on shaping his athletes for the future.
(Photo courtesy of the University of Iowa Sports Information Department.)

Naturally, there are a lot of ways to look at things, and a good coach should try to direct his athletes toward making healthy choices. "Our sport affects people for a lifetime. Coaches are influential and have the chance to do good things for other people. When I look back on my 21 years of coaching, I know that there are a lot of wins and there are losses there, too. I don't focus on that. I look at the effect I had on the athletes, and I like to see what they took with them from my program," he said.

As a coach, Gable strived to get his athletes and assistant coaches on the same wavelength. That wavelength, of course, was designed by Gable and set at a high standard.

"When you have leaders, then you're in good shape. You need the team to function so that if the coach doesn't show up, the team still knows what to do," he said. "Just because you had success as a wrestler doesn't mean you will automatically make a good coach. You may have done it, but it's different when you have to get kids to want to do it. If you get all fired up about a recruiting class, then you're never going to make it. You have to be fired up about your seniors because they are your leaders."

As an ambassador to the sport, Gable's focus is on the direction that wrestling is taking. There are 250,000 high school wrestlers in the United States. That number drops to 7,500 wrestlers competing in 275 programs at the collegiate level. The number of wrestlers who take it to the ultimate step—competing at the Olympics—is only 500. Or, to look at it another way, 7 percent of Americans are involved in wrestling.

"Thinking about that kind of difference with those kinds of numbers is wild. I wonder what happened. Where did all those wrestlers go? People drop off and change focus, but that's a lot of people," he said.

Not for a minute, though, will Gable let that lingering thought turn into a negative one. He is busy exploring ways to enhance the sport. He is not one for waiting until tomorrow to get something done. He believes that "the current is good because now is when it's happening."

"Look at the room we have to grow. Look at what we could have. There are a lot of people out there who have been affected in some way by wrestling. There are over twenty million people associated with wrestling. When you talk to people who have wrestled, they all

University of Iowa coach Dan Gable often had reason to celebrate as he led his Hawkeyes to 15 national titles in 21 seasons.
(Photo courtesy of the University of Iowa Sports Information Department.)

say that the impact it had on their lives is huge. These are the people we need to reach out to and ask them to step up for the sport," he said.

"In Iran wrestling is like a religion, and it's the national sport in Mongolia. In our country, a high percentage of people who have wrestled are in the leadership divisions in our government," he said.

He knows from experience that wrestlers learn to function at a level others don't even know about. "Once you've wrestled, it helps you to contend with life issues. It helps you to deal with things. If you have a coach who knows how to train, then you will be taxed and pushed to another level. You have to be disciplined in so many avenues. You have to love every aspect of it. I loved the battles with weight loss and injuries. It all became part of the task. How am I going to handle this? How am I going to work through this? I know I am an extreme, but it can be done," he said.

When it comes to getting it done, Gable worked at a fanatical pace to achieve what he did in his career. He would work out to the point of complete exhaustion and coached so passionately that he admits he once passed out by the end of a match. How does a person who functions at this level keep it going?

"You definitely have to work in your recovery time or you'll burn out fast. My recovery, on a daily basis, is just as important as the workout itself. There are things that a person can do in a recovery that help them to get ready to come back and do it all over again. I trained my athletes so that they could return to the mat and go full speed again and again and again," he said.

Gable says that he believes in using some massage technique, hot and cold therapies, and extra communication. "These are little things from a motivational point of view. It helps to stay one extra hour after practice to learn how to recover. Communication is important. Sometimes just sitting in a sauna and talking or thinking about what took place in the last two hours at practice is all it takes," he said.

For a high school wrestler, the recovery focus should be on nutrition, homework, and the proper amount of sleep. Recovery time can be enhanced by eliminating extra distractions such as video games and sitting in front of a computer.

"You have to have a routine. You have to feel good about what you're doing or you won't do it well. You'll be tired before it starts," Gable said. "I think the parents, coaches, and teachers need to read the situation and then help the athlete make the judgments. It's

important to know they're headed in the right direction. You can't lay out a lesson plan or practice plan for two months straight. You don't know how it's going to go until you're actually going through it. You need your guidelines, but you need to adjust. A coach has to make intelligent decisions for his athletes."

Gable believes it is important for younger athletes to be involved in activities besides wrestling. Once a person can draw from other sports and activities, then they can weigh the importance of where wrestling fits into the picture. "You need to choose what you really want to do. I was training my whole life for my profession, but I didn't know it. If you do things right, you'll have success. The kids who didn't make the grade on the mat used the tools they learned in wrestling to make the grade in life," he said.

Gable recalls that his parents were very supportive of his involvement in wrestling. "They never said do this or do that, but they were there for me. They supported my efforts in different ways. For my birthday they gave me a small wrestling mat. For Christmas they gave me weights. They offered guidance, not demands," he said.

Gable has said, on more than one occasion, that America needs wrestling. He thinks that wrestling makes such an impact on individual lives that if more people become involved with the sport, then there could be positive differences being made within the country.

"America needs wrestling because wrestling is a standard of excellence. America needs wrestling because it teaches discipline. You want freedom and you want a high ideal, which comes at a price. The more wrestling there is throughout our country, the better we will be as a nation," Gable said. "When people are put into positions of leadership and they don't apply the process that you can learn through wrestling, then you're basically holding the world back."

4

No Elbows, No Knees, No Excuses

Kyle Maynard,
Author and Motivational Speaker

Kyle Maynard is a rare breed. The epic story of Maynard is one of the most inspirational tales of the modern day. A congenital amputee, Maynard is a young man who was born with arms that end before his elbows and legs that end before his knees. Despite his apparent disability, Maynard has used his passion for wrestling to excel.

In an age where the slightest disfigurement has landed many people in a plastic surgeon's office, this is the story of one young man who learned to play the cards he was dealt in a game where winner takes all. That game, of course, is *life*.

Physicians are not sure exactly how many babies are born each year with some form of congenital amputation. What doctors do know is that the birth defects are caused by fibrous bands that constrict the membrane that holds the fetus, which results in pinching off developing extremities. Most often these birth defects result in a baby without a finger or a toe; Maynard's form was extreme. In his case, this genetic fluke came out of nowhere. Despite the initial shock and dismay, in the eyes of Scott and Anita Maynard, Kyle's parents, they had their firstborn—a beautiful baby boy.

Maynard was born on March 24, 1986, in Fort Wayne, Indiana, into a loving home where his parents raised him on the No Excuses Principle. This principle would be the key to unlocking Maynard's gumption to excel, first with the little things and then with the bigger things. In the early days, he learned to eat, dress himself, write, type, and drive a car without hands or legs and without prosthetics. In the later days, his competitive spirit took over. He was a nose tackle on the youth football team, which led him to discover his life's passion—wrestling.

Kyle Maynard (right) with his friend Cael Sanderson, who won an Olympic gold medal in 2004 in Athens.
(Photo courtesy of Kyle Maynard.)

"Without a doubt, wrestling saved my life. I have seen other kids in my situation where they were born without limbs, and there are high suicide rates and high instances of obesity. It is so easy to give up on life. For me, wrestling had the answers I needed. I will continue with it in some way for the rest of my life because it keeps me in shape both mentally and physically," Maynard explained.

His triumph as a top state wrestler in Georgia, where his family had relocated before fifth grade, was the direct result of the No Excuses Principle. Maynard encountered compassionate high school coach Cliff Ramos, who welcomed the opportunity to instruct Maynard and accepted the challenge of creating new ways to teach techniques that traditionally require the use of hands and legs. It took a while before a successful strategy was developed. In fact, the journey to placing in the states was filled with its share of heartache.

"I had to learn that strength doesn't get you everywhere in wrestling. I had to figure a lot of things out. If I was going for wrist control, I had to lock it up with my shoulder and chin. I had a lot of speed, too. My strength was when I learned how to out-finesse guys," he said.

For the longest stretch of time, his athletic prospects seemed futile. He went 0-35 in competition. But his father reassured him that this is how many first-year wrestlers start out, and Maynard kept his sights on making daily improvements.

"I learned so much about life from wrestling. There is nothing easy about wrestling, but I learned that the more you sacrifice, the better the rewards are," he said.

The challenge that Maynard faced was unprecedented; no other wrestler with his degree of handicap had ever attempted to compete. He designed some specialty moves with the help of his coach such as the jaw-breaker, the peek-out, and the buzz-saw. He earned a starting spot as a 103-pounder at Collins Hill High School in Suwanee, Georgia.

"For me, I'm a competitor. That's where my passion is. I like to get out there and compete. That's where my heart is," he said. "I thank God for the blessings in my life, especially the blessings that came through the sport."

Compete is exactly what Maynard did. In his senior season he went 35-16 and was one of the top high school wrestlers in Georgia.

He qualified for and competed in the 2004 Georgia High School Wrestling Championships. He narrowly missed All-American status at the National High School Coaches Association (NHSCA) Senior National Wrestling Championships.

"I had a successful senior year. We had a tough schedule, and I beat some tough guys. In the state team tournament, a kid came crashing down on my face with his forearm and I broke my nose. My wrestling style is such that I use my head as a battering ram and using a mask didn't work so I went without it, but it made for a tough end to a great season. I gave up going out with friends and watching TV for two months so that I could train. I have no regrets training like that," he said.

Maynard still loves to train, and he competes on the club team at the University of Georgia. He also has stepped a few feet outside the traditional wrestling community as he is learning "catch wrestling"— a submission-style wrestling that draws from Brazilian jiu-jitsu. In the midst of adjusting to college life where he lives in a regular dormitory and has roommates and all the distractions of that environment, Maynard decided to write a book about his life that he appropriately titled *No Excuses*. He cranked out the 55,000-word memoir in a rapid four and a half months while pursuing a full college course load. The book is an honest account straight from his heart that is loaded with inspiration and insight. Maynard wrote it hoping to inspire a few people. The reality is that *No Excuses* hit the *New York Times* bestselling hardcover nonfiction list in 2005, and now Maynard is traveling around the country speaking to people in sales groups in large corporations and to college and high school students. There are some weeks where he has to fit in three or four speaking engagements in different parts of the country.

"That, I have to say, was a very cool feeling," Maynard said about his book making the bestseller list. "I made the time to write the book. I set my schedule up so that Tuesday through Thursday I went to school and then Saturday through Monday I put in 18-hour days writing. The thing with writing is that sometimes it flows and sometimes there's nothing. There was a little procrastination in there. My editor taught me how to set goals and go for it. My goal was to write around 12,000 to 15,000 words per week," Maynard explained.

Before he started his writing project, he made sure he finished his freshman wrestling season at Georgia where the club team packs a

serious schedule, taking on other local Division I programs. At the end of the 2005 season, Maynard tested his weight-lifting skills and broke the world record for modified bench press by lifting 360 pounds, three times his body weight.

When Regnery Publishing approached Maynard to write a book, he thought it was an interesting idea. He had hopes that if he shared his story, it might help some people. He was aware of the concept of "ghostwriters" and figured that's how this would work.

"The publisher was excited about the idea of doing a book so my story could be told. I was talking about the idea with my dad, and he said that I should be the one to write it because I know the subject matter the best. So that's what I did," he said.

Meanwhile, Maynard is enjoying his 15 minutes of fame, as he modestly calls this response to his story going public. He is a handsome, buff college student whose good looks have graced the cover of *Vanity Fair*, appeared in *GQ*, and been in an Abercrombie & Fitch ad. He makes no attempt to hide his disfigurement; in fact, it doesn't really seem to faze him.

"There are a lot of people who view disabled people as inferior. They think that disabled people are of no use. I think everyone is disabled in one way or another. My disability just happens to be very obvious," he said.

As accomplished as Maynard is, he still finds it difficult to believe how some people react to him.

"The airport personnel are used to me by now because I am traveling all over the place all the time. It amazes me that they know how capable I am of doing things for myself, yet they still are trying to buckle me and stuff," he said.

Interestingly, while there were many people who supported Maynard's wrestling quest, there were plenty of critics along the way. Some people felt that Maynard was at an unfair advantage because he has the torso and strength of a much heavier wrestler, but he weighed in at 103 pounds in high school because of the absence of legs and arms.

"I've encountered all sorts of people and they say stuff without thinking. Some people really don't know what to make of it. My dad was videotaping one of my high school matches and this guy walks up to him while he's filming and starts making all these comments about how I shouldn't be allowed to wrestle. We have the whole con-

versation on tape. He's saying, 'Hey, that kid shouldn't be out there!' It's amazing the way people think," Maynard said.

What's truly amazing is the way Maynard thinks. He turns negative comments and long stares from strangers into self-motivation.

"Anytime anyone doubted me or said that I couldn't do something, I just fed off it. It motivates me. There is nothing that I am hindered from doing. The feedback that I get has been great," he said.

For example, two badly wounded soldiers returned from Iraq. Both felt saddled by their injuries and refused to speak to other people. They happened to see the "Larry King Live" show that featured Maynard; the next day they got up and went to rehab.

"I am blessed that I have a gift to help people. There are always more ways to help other people. I try to leave a lasting impression. I look at the big picture and set big goals for myself. I don't let obstacles keep me from my dreams," he said.

Maynard redirects his own passion for wrestling and fitness into inspiring other people, especially young wrestlers. He believes strongly about what wrestling can do for a person.

"When I speak to groups of young wrestlers, I tell them that if they push themselves and stay with it, wrestling can prepare you for dealing with life. There is constant pressure when a person enters the working world. The correlation between wrestling and what happens in the real world can't be denied. There are so many wrestlers who go on to be extremely successful," he said.

Maynard doesn't feel he needs to solve everyone's problems, and he tries to avoid people who have a tendency to be constantly negative.

"I think you can sit around and complain all the time, or you can get up and do something. I see kids who are wasting time at school with partying too much. They're losing sight of what it's all about. They have to make a decision to get up and do something with their lives. It's not my responsibility to get involved with every person because I know I have my own improvements that I need to make for myself. I just try to lead by example," he said.

So what lies ahead for Maynard?

"Well, I've been touring on and off now for about two years. I'm happy about being busy with that. I hope in the future that I will always be involved in wrestling. I've thought about opening fitness centers. Truthfully, though, I've got my schedule blocked off through this spring, and beyond that, who knows? The book contract literally happened overnight. Things seem to happen so rapidly in my life. Right now I feel I want to still be involved in the sport in some way," Maynard said.

Maynard's iron will is the result of living his motto—"It's not what I *can* do, but what I *will* do." ESPN awarded him an ESPY as Best Athlete with a Disability in 2004. He has also been featured on "The Oprah Winfrey Show," "Larry King Live," and "Good Morning, America." In 2005, he received the Medal of Courage from the National Wrestling Hall of Fame. Maynard has been honored by the Georgia chapter of the National Wrestling Hall of Fame as well as the Georgia State Wrestling Hall of Fame. He also has received the President's Award for Courage from the Humanitarian Hall of Fame.

5
The Code of Coaching Ethics

Coach Terry Brands, U.S. Olympic Freestyle Wrestling

It was early October 2005 and most folks had not yet picked their pumpkins or set the mums out on the front steps. Terry Brands's two children took delight in an early season snowfall that dumped itself on Colorado. Brands had just left his coaching job at the University of Tennessee at Chattanooga and moved his family to Colorado to coach the USA Olympic freestyle wrestling team.

"This is so exciting for us. We didn't have any of this when we were in Chattanooga. My kids are going crazy with this

Terry Brands moved to Colorado to coach the U.S. Olympic freestyle team. (Photo courtesy of USA Wrestling.)

snow. It's so great," said Brands. He loves this new challenge, and he is happy to see his children and wife enjoying their new venture together in Colorado.

Although Brands is inundated with work and new responsibilities at the Olympic training center, he took the time to share his ideas about his life's passion: wrestling.

"I think that as a coach, you have to practice what you preach. You have to have high morals and integrity in everything that you do. Coaches need to behave professionally at all times," he said. "Wrestlers will naturally gravitate to a coach that shows these qualities."

As with most aspects of Brands's life, he takes a no-nonsense, intensely deep, focused approach to coaching. He believes you not only have to teach a positive lifestyle, but you have to live it yourself. Brands recognized that the toughness he developed in the wrestling room has helped him with how he acts in his marriage, at work, and in his role as a parent.

"I think that wrestling makes everything in life easier to deal with. It is a sport that teaches you to draw from your strength. How do you

deal with some of the terrible things that happen in life? Wrestling really prepares a person to deal with the tough things," he said.

Some of the tough things in life stem from what today's society is open to. Brands has deep concerns about the youth of America, with their access to pornography on the Internet and the ability to form loose relationships through the computer. He is also concerned about inappropriate subject matter on television as well as the prevalence of drugs and alcohol. He believes a coach has to step forward and be a mentor to all of the athletes in his program.

"Before you leave the practice room each night, you have to know that you did something to help each wrestler. You can't let anything slide. You need to hold yourself accountable. You have to ask yourself, 'Did I do the right thing?' I think a lot about this and it usually hits me when I go to bed at night," he said.

Brands has an All-American perspective when it comes to his coaching. Noting that this country was founded on great philosophies and Christian moral values, he said we should all take a few lessons from the founding fathers.

"They went out there with their ragtag army and came back victorious. If you think about the militiamen from the 13 colonies, they had some will to fight and win. It's great when you think about it," he said.

Honesty is a key ingredient in creating a winning wrestling program. Here are a few questions Brands poses to wrestling coaches:

1. Are you staying 100 percent current with the sport?
2. Are you doing the right things with the club money?
3. Are you giving up some of your personal time to assist the development of the program?
4. Do you instill enough trust that the athletes will be allowed to accompany you on a road trip?

Brands says that coaches at every level of wrestling, from youth club programs right up through Olympic level teams, need to adhere to the same coaching ethics.

"Don't cheat any part of the system. Don't turn a blind eye to any detail. Every coach has a responsibility to stay current with the sport

and to give 100 percent to each person in the program. Ultimately, if you cheat the system, then you cheat your country. It's as basic as that," he said.

When Brands talks about wrestling, it is obvious that this is not just a job or career for him, it is his passion. While the sport can seem overwhelming at times, his advice to coaches and wrestlers is to take one day at a time. His prescription for success is to focus on doing the best that you can do today and don't worry about what may or may not happen three weeks from now. Every coach needs to set priorities, which should include building a lot of family time into every day.

"I set my priorities. My goal is to be the best husband, the best father, and the best coach that I can be," he said.

Brands will not push his own son, Nelson, into wrestling, although it is only natural that he will be exposed to the sport. He has seen many examples of overzealous parents forcing their children into sports.

"This sport is way too hard, so an athlete has to be into it. A kid has to get up and say, 'I want to wrestle.' Too many parents think they need to start the kids competitively at four or five years old. The truth is, only a small percentage become Olympians. Parents should not live vicariously through their children. My parents never pushed me, just supported me. There's a big difference there. My mom never asked if I worked out. She never forced us to go to tournaments. It came from within. I wanted to do it. I wanted to make it happen," he said.

The coach has a major responsibility to motivate the athletes in the wrestling room. A coach can deal with the team as a whole by putting them through the same workout session in the wrestling room.

Although he has to deal with the team as a whole, a successful coach also has to find what works best for each individual. If a coach knows that certain individuals enjoy the weight room or enjoy drilling, then it is possible to challenge them individually in those specific areas. This, of course, can be very frustrating because it is a process that does not happen overnight. It can often take three years to see a significant transformation in a wrestler.

"As a coach you need to get into their heads. You have to get them to realize that they need to take advantage of their God-given talents. There's no room for laziness. It's not an easy job because you have 35 athletes that you need to figure out, and it's not all about wrestling. There are academics, workouts, social pressures, and family life. You have to get your kids on the right track. I have found that if you show your kids that you care about them as a person—and not just as a wrestler—then they trust you and that is huge," he said.

One of the approaches to creating team unity is through "gut-busting" workouts. Brands likes to hammer the basics, outwork the world, and train his team to be the best. He explained, "Everyone is gunning for the same championship. It boils down to how you go about getting there that makes the difference. When you have 35 guys going through the same gut-busting workout, you build something there."

In the wrestling room, Brands finds the hardest-working wrestler in the room and praises his work ethic as a positive example for the team. With that approach, he feels that the other wrestlers will then want to work that hard. A coach needs to keep negativity in check and be sure never to single out someone lacking in skill or motivation.

"You never want to tell a kid that his technique stinks," Brands advised. "Instead, tell him what areas he needs to work harder in. It is a never-ending process because there is always room for improvement."

It is a coach's responsibility to get involved as a mentor but not as a friend. There are clear boundaries, and it is important not to lose sight of your role as a coach. You can't allow yourself to become overly involved, but you still need to show that you care.

Brands will not compromise his work ethic for anything. When it comes to a coach addressing the student in the student-athlete, he makes sure his athletes know that education comes first. He tells his wrestlers that you can't make it in this country without an education. If a wrestler is struggling in school, then the coach should try to help him to find a way to do better. Brands feels that students should earn a minimum of a B average; nothing less is acceptable.

"If a wrestler is performing at 85 percent, which is a B average, then he is probably not having a very good season, right? So why would it be acceptable to go below that academically? To excel in school, you just have to go to class, pay attention, and do your homework. If you struggle with your schoolwork, then get yourself extra help. That's the basic message kids need reinforced."

Brands recognizes that some student-athletes have learning disabilities and encourages coaches to help find the proper placements for these students so that they can succeed academically.

"It is so important for students not to get in the habit of using their disabilities as a crutch. They need to deal with what they have been dealt in life. A coach should look to help in every way he can and not turn a blind eye to academic issues. Don't give these kids the easy way out. There is always a way to make it work," he said.

Now, as Brands travels to new corners of the world with the Olympic men's freestyle wrestling team, he takes with him a lifetime of figuring out ways to make things work.

"The window of opportunity in wrestling is so small that if you want to accomplish your goals, well, then you better get busy," he said.

6
Making the Grade

Coach Jay Weiss, Harvard University; Coach Brendan Buckley, Columbia University

When wrestlers apply in the classroom the same work ethic they use on the mat, the results are typically outstanding. The combination of excelling as a student and as a wrestler can be the key that opens the doors into some of the most elite universities in the world.

"I think that being a top-notch student and a top-notch wrestler can improve your chances of getting into some of the toughest schools," said Jay Weiss, head coach at Harvard University.

Once a wrestler is accepted into an elite school, however, the real work begins.

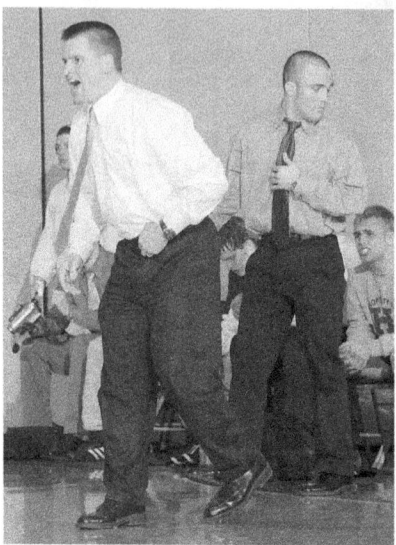

Harvard coach Jay Weiss encourages his wrestlers to pursue their academics with the same intensity they put forth in wrestling.
(Photo courtesy of Harvard University Sports Information Department.)

Columbia coach Brendan Buckley likes to see his wrestlers apply the lessons learned in the sport to their academic pursuits.
(Photo courtesy of Columbia University Sports Information Department.)

"It's very difficult to balance the sport and the academics. The people that we recruit have juggled this in the past, but what they have to do when they come to Harvard is re-start because the demands are so high. I find that they are talented people who are being highly challenged in the classroom and in the wrestling room," Weiss said.

Columbia University coach Brendan Buckley also deals with wrestlers who make the grade on and off the mat.

"Philosophically, I've seen wrestlers who have been able to apply the lessons learned in the sport to their academic pursuits, and it has opened up a world of opportunities," Buckley said. "More specifically, wrestling has opened up doors to top-notch academic schools. If you look at the national rankings, you'll see that the Ivy League wrestlers are producing at the national level. As a coach, I feel proud that I get to help influence and shape my wrestlers."

Harvard wrestler Jesse Jantzen is a classic example of what an Ivy League wrestler can do. In 2004, Jantzen (149 pounds) became the second wrestler since 1938 to win a national championship for Harvard. He also won the Outstanding Wrestler Award at the tournament.

"I definitely think that my talent in wrestling helped me get into Harvard. I had good grades, but it helps to have something else that you excel in," Jantzen said. The academic regimen was extremely challenging, but he worked hard to balance academics and athletics.

"For me, I had to stay on a strict schedule and I always had to plan ahead. The traveling and competitions really forced me to coordinate my efforts. The professors were reasonable. I had to approach my professors and discuss my schedule so they could give me assignments ahead of time," Jantzen said.

Harvard qualified three other wrestlers to the NCAA championships in 2004 with Max Meltzer (third at 141), Reggie Lee (third at 197), and Bode Ogunwole (third at HWT).

"I was so happy for Jesse. I know what he went through to get there. He put himself in that position. That moment when he won it was tops for me in my coaching career, that's for sure," Weiss said.

When Weiss took over Harvard's struggling program, he knew he needed a better foundation for his program. "I knew that I couldn't just put Band-Aids on things, and I really wanted the wrestlers to see the value in the whole wrestling experience. The sport is much more

Jesse Jantzen celebrates his 2004 NCAA championship with Harvard coach Jay Weiss.
(Photo courtesy of Harvard University Sports Information Department.)

The Harvard University Wrestling Team Mission Statement

The Harvard wrestling team provides an opportunity for students to fully develop the values on which this university rests: the advancement of knowledge to the highest potential. The purpose of the wrestling family is to develop a unit that transcends the walls of this university, to provide the necessary tools for the pursuit of individual and team goals, and to recognize this activity from a larger community perspective. Harvard Wrestling strives to be more than a team. Rather, the focus is to be a home away from home. The family is critical in providing encouragement, understanding, and personal growth during the undergraduate's four years at Harvard. The Harvard wrestler gains satisfaction from knowing that he did his best to become the best that he is capable of becoming.

than takedowns and back points. What you learn in wrestling, you'll use for the rest of your life," Weiss said.

Weiss designed a team mission statement with the help of his wrestlers. The purpose of the mission statement is to keep the athletes focused on the same course throughout the season. All wrestlers agree on the mission statement and strive to meet its goals.

"We kept tweaking it until we had it right. When things get tough during the season, we go back to it and read it. We all find it to be so helpful. There's so much to gain from wrestling," Weiss said.

Jantzen was happy with his overall Harvard experience, and he speaks highly of his coach. "Coach Weiss was a perfect fit for me. He was like a father figure. He gets to know his athletes on a personal level, and he takes a big interest in you. He's a super guy."

Buckley feels that when a person combines academic talent with wrestling, it sets him up for success during college and in the years after graduation. "When I get feedback from wrestlers who have graduated, the most common statement is that no one in their field works as hard as they do. Wrestlers are willing to work above and beyond what their colleagues can do time and time again," he said.

> Within the realm of diverse individual goals, our common mission shall be advanced through desire, discipline, and determination. Our program recognizes these virtues to be essential in the mental and physical development of its members and their roles as Harvard wrestlers, students, and, more important, as life's citizens of this world. Leadership development is of utmost importance as one navigates through his years here on campus.
>
> Through these means, Harvard wrestling strives to paint its masterpiece on a larger canvas. A graduate of this program will acquire the appropriate tools to navigate through the often sharp curves of life. The acquisition of perspective is the inevitable outcome of the journey, made up of blood, sweat, and tears.
>
> Entering for the love of wrestling, one will leave with an appreciation for life.

As enthusiastic coaches, both Buckley and Weiss enjoy hearing from former wrestlers who have graduated and moved on to make contributions to society.

"Many of my former wrestlers are doing great. Some have gone on to medical school and law school. There is a first lieutenant in the Navy who did two tours in Iraq. I'm amazed at what they're doing after they leave. It's humbling to me because I have them for four years and then they're off," Weiss said. "While I have them, though, I encourage them to take advantage of what Harvard's mission is—teaching individuals to go out and do many different things very well."

Princeton assistant coach Ryan Bonfiglio is a former 165-pound Tiger wrestler who captained the team in 2000 and 2001. Bonfiglio placed second in the Eastern Intercollegiate Wrestling Association (EIWA) and qualified for the Nationals his senior year. He was a chemistry major who chose Princeton for its academics and then decided to wrestle once he was there.

"It was difficult in the beginning because I found myself thrown into tough classes and thrown into tough competition all at once," Bonfiglio explained. "You have to figure out how to balance everything and make the right choices for yourself."

Bonfiglio discovered that he performed better academically when he was involved in wrestling than in the off-season. "I knew I had to fit in practice and studying, so there was no room for too many extra things," he said.

Princeton has a lightweight football team that he played on during his senior year because Bonfiglio loved the life of the student-athlete. "Academics are the top priority at Princeton and the coaches here recognize that," he said. "I enjoyed having the ability to work hard and stay focused. Princeton has 250 years of history and being affiliated with this school has been one of the most fulfilling experiences."

7
As Good as It Gets

Stephen Neal,
New England Patriots

It was early in the New England Patriots' 2005–2006 season when the two-time NFL defending champions were gearing up for a possible three-peat. Offensive lineman Stephen Neal was playing in his backyard with his daughter at his Massachusetts home and thinking about the Patriots' chances of making the playoffs. His focus shifted to his daughter, who squealed with delight as she jumped into a pile of leaves on a gorgeous Indian summer afternoon. Neal relished the time he was spending with his family.

"This is as good as it gets," he said.

He sincerely means it.

When you stop to *talk* with Neal, you can't help but think he is just a regular guy. But when you stop to *think* about Neal, he is far from regular. He spends most of his time these days protecting New England quarterback Tom Brady from the pass rush and opening running lanes for running back Corey Dillon, all without ever having played football in college.

Flash forward to mid-January 2006. The Patriots secured their fourth playoff berth in five seasons before the Denver Broncos ended New England's run for its fourth Super Bowl title in five years. Neal was a major factor in the offensive attack every step of the way.

Neal's journey to the NFL and to being a starting lineman for three Super Bowl champion New England Patriot teams began on the wrestling mat. That is where he developed into a champion under the guidance of Coach T. J. Kerr at California State University, Bakersfield. Neal claimed two NCAA heavyweight championships in 1998 and 1999 and finished his collegiate career with a 156-10-0 record. Then he became the 1999 World Freestyle Champion as a heavyweight and he was named the FILA (Fédération Internationnal

Offensive guard Stephen Neal (#61) has protected quarterback Tom Brady through three Super Bowl victories.
(Photo courtesy of New England Patriots Public Relations.)

Stephen Neal was a two-time NCAA champion for Cal State Bakersfield where he compiled a career record of 156-10-0.
(Photo courtesy of Cal State Bakersfield Sports Information Department.)

de Lutte Amateur) International Freestyle Wrestler of the Year. He was also the 1999 recipient of the Dan Hodge Award and won a gold medal at the 1999 Pan American Games in Winnipeg, Canada.

"I have to say that wrestling definitely taught me my work ethic. I never expect anything but the best from myself," he said. "When I was at Bakersfield, it was all about doing better and setting higher goals. Wrestling opened me up to believing that goals can be reached and dreams do come true."

Neal explained that if he beat an opponent by five points, then the next time he faced that opponent he wanted to improve and beat him by more points. He adopted the philosophy that you have to improve every day or else you might weaken. His practice philosophy paid off as he won five matches in the 1999 World Championship where he defeated Andrei Shumilin of Russia 4–3 in the final match for the gold medal.

"Wrestling taught me that hard work and consistency pay off. That, right there, are the keys to being successful in everything you do in life. Whether it's your job, your marriage, or raising your children, you need to be consistent and work hard at it. Nothing ever comes easy, and you shouldn't expect it to," Neal said. He added, "No matter how good you are and no matter what level athlete you are, you can't get complacent. You don't want your opponent to work harder than you or get better than you."

Legendary wrestler and former Iowa coach Dan Gable worked with Neal on his way to winning the World Championship. "Stephen Neal's story is great because it is the perfect example of what our sport can do for you when you move into other areas. It's amazing what can happen when you apply wrestling to another avenue. Do you think a football player could turn around and become the best wrestler?" Gable said.

Ben Peterson, 1972 Olympic gold medalist, enjoyed watching Neal at the World Championship. "I was with him before he won the World Championship. He's like a little boy with a new toy. He's always got this big grin going. His spirit is great. I sat with his wife and his daughter when he won in New York. It was great to see him win it," Peterson remarked.

Peterson is also an advocate of football players pursuing wrestling. He comes from a large family of wrestlers and football players. "If you want to succeed in football, then you better get yourself on the

wrestling mat. Everything you learn in wrestling translates to the football field. Stephen Neal is proof of that," he said.

When Coach Kerr reflects on his three decades of collegiate coaching, he says coaching Neal is the highlight. He talks about Neal with such pride and admiration, not because of his accomplishments, but because of the tremendous person that he is.

"He is unbelievable. He is a great guy. I call him every week. I stay in touch so that I can support him. He is a very lucky person, but he earned that luck," Kerr said.

Neal is the product of a supportive family who encouraged him to pursue wrestling at Cal State Bakersfield. The university was close to his home in San Diego, and his parents wanted to watch him wrestle. Their support started years earlier when the ninth-grade football season was over and his friend said he should try wrestling.

"My friend told me that wrestling is the toughest sport. I said there was no way it was tougher than football. He challenged me to try it. I did and discovered wrestling is the toughest sport. I didn't like it at first. I didn't like getting put on my back and fighting from there. My dad was a basketball player, but then he got fired up about the idea of me wrestling. He took me to Los Angeles for tournaments. I loved spending that time with him. It was very enjoyable and very special. Great things happened because of wrestling," Neal said.

Neal uses many of his wrestling skills in football. In wrestling he never wanted to give up any points or get reversed. He focused on being perfect. His mind-set in football reflects that same edge. "I don't want to lose any battles out there. I want to win every run block and every pass block," he said.

While both sports are great, Neal explained that it's tough to draw comparisons between wrestling and football. "Wrestling is the ultimate one-to-one battle of you versus him. Winning the World Championship was great because it was an individual thing. In football, there are two head coaches working their strategies like in a chess match. When we won the Super Bowl, there was an entire team to celebrate with because there were a lot of guys in on it. Both were great experiences," he said.

Although Neal wrestled well in high school in San Diego, his skills were still pretty raw when he entered Bakersfield.

"When he came to us we told him he should be a heavyweight. He had no technique, just blood and guts. He would dive on his knees

Stephen Neal looks to win every run block or pass block play.
(Photo courtesy of New England Patriots Public Relations.)

and use his length to suck the guy up into a double. He got beat up in the beginning, but that didn't last long. I made him eat and got 15 pounds on him. He got more athletic, too. He developed his own double leg," Kerr said.

A typical Neal match was unusual for a heavyweight, because he pushed his way into position for headlocks. His quickness and power enabled him to beat his opponents once he had them on the mat.

"Sometimes you have to wake up the sleeping giant. We would work the heck out of him, give him two days of rest, and then send him out to compete—and he loved it. He could look at things and see what he had to do. He pinned everyone from his feet," Kerr said.

When the Patriots went to the Super Bowl, Neal invited Kerr to share the experience. Neal speaks of his college coach with great respect. "He's such a great guy. They don't make too many people like him. He's been a role model to me," Neal said.

Kerr went to the brunch in the players' hotel before the game and said the event was incredible. "We're used to seeing him in the NFL now. His whole story is unbelievable," Kerr said.

Lehigh University coach Greg Strobel was in the coaches' corner when Neal won the World Championship. He also feels privileged

for having the opportunity to work with Neal. "He is an incredible athlete with such a sense of can-do. That's the mark of a champion," Strobel said. "He was pretty cool about his final match of the World Championship. At the break the coaches told him that he wasn't going to beat this guy on technique so he had to turn it into an athletic event. We made a plan, and he had the ability to follow the plan and do it athletically. He's a gifted athlete."

In the off-season, Neal happily returns to Bakersfield where he is the strength-training coach for the wrestling team. "He comes back to help out. He enjoys when he is back in this world," Kerr said.

Not only does Neal love returning to California, but he enjoys the opportunity to encourage others in wrestling.

"The thing with wrestling is that there are no financial rewards that exist in other sports like football, basketball, and baseball. Wrestlers can't get distracted by that. This sport is not designed to be glamorous. It's not like 'Sports Center' is big on covering wrestling," Neal laughed about the sport's lack of publicity. "The focus needs to be on what you learn from wrestling. The lessons and discipline are the rewards. Once a wrestler realizes that, then great things can happen."

Things like Super Bowl rings and World Championships . . . that's as good as it gets.

Stephen Neal's Favorite Drill

Level Change

"My favorite wrestling drill is a level-changing drill. This can be done by yourself or with a partner. Basically, I get in my wrestling stance and do head fakes or tap my partner's (or shadow partner's) head. Then when the opponent straightens his legs or stands up, I change levels and get into a position to attack. This drill helped me a great deal when I was wrestling. When your opponent gets into bad position, the only way to take advantage of the situation is to get in an attack mode. If you are not in good position, you can't score."

8
Promoting Your Program

Coach J Robinson, University of Minnesota

When it comes to promoting a wrestling program, Coach J Robinson is a mastermind. He says he takes a close look around him, sees what works, and then makes it happen for his University of Minnesota wrestling program.

"You don't have to reinvent the wheel with promoting your program. You can follow the lead of other major sports and pirate the good ideas. Just look at football or look at basketball and watch what they do. You take that and apply it to your

program. The biggest mistake a lot of coaches make is waiting for someone else to promote your program. It's not going to happen," he said. "You have to get it done."

When Minnesota had a big dual meet with Iowa, Robinson decided to increase the price of the tickets because that is what the football team did and it made some money for the program.

"We're competing for the entertainment value of the family. Is a family going out to spend money on a movie or a wrestling match? We made it so that Minnesota wrestling is an event now. You can take your wife out to dinner and go to the match, where you have a reserved seat. Then there's a function after it. That's entertainment and more people need to see it that way," he explained.

So how did Robinson create this atmosphere?

"People go to football games because it's a social event and they have an excuse to tailgate. Wrestling programs need to be promoted in such a way that the people get more than just wrestling when they go to a match. I think there has to be a halftime at wrestling matches. There's a halftime in every sport. That's fan friendly, so we do it, too. We bring in halftime entertainment for fans to watch. It really adds to the experience."

Another idea Robinson borrowed from other sports programs is the concept of a printed program filled with information about the home team, the opponent, and what is happening with wrestling around the country.

"We have a 16-page program that we sell, and it is loaded with information. We make more money on our program than most teams in the country make at the gate in ticket sales. We publish it ourselves, and people buy it so that they know what is going on in wrestling. It's all about creating an expectation when the fan comes."

Many wrestling coaches don't publish an event program or put together wrestling socials after matches simply because they don't have to. It is not listed in their job descriptions, so they don't do it. Why should a coach look to do promotional things?

"Well, first, it helps to get the word out about wrestling being a great spectator sport and it generates interest. Second, some of the things produce revenue, which generates into power. The finances give you more options in your program."

When Robinson first started coaching at Minnesota, ticket sales totaled about $5,000. At that time it cost the athletic department the

Promoting Your Program

same amount of money to work the match. The athletic department told him they wanted to let people in for free and not staff the event anymore. Robinson took a different perspective.

"I looked at the sport as a rare commodity that needed to be marketed. I went back to the athletic department and said to them that we would handle everything independently, and we would keep what we made at the gate. It was a win-win situation. They saved $5,000 and we could make some money for the program by staffing the event ourselves. Each year ticket sales increased until we were making $200,000, and then the athletic department decided to take it back."

One of the promotional themes Robinson has created is hometown night, where people from all around Minnesota cheer for their hometown wrestler. Other themes are alumni night and bring a friend night. When Minnesota wrestled Iowa in a big dual meet, the attendance was a record-breaking 15,500 people. The event was staged at an off-campus venue where there were seats that went right up to the mat, pre-match video highlights, instant replay, pyrotechnics, and even waiter service to bring food and drinks to the seats.

"It's a great idea to sell reserved seats because people are willing to pay a few extra dollars for an assigned seat. It prevents people from

Left: University of Minnesota coach J Robinson masterfully promotes his wrestling program.

Above: Coach Robinson offers words of encouragement during a match.

(Photos courtesy of University of Minnesota Sports Information Department.)

having to sit in bleacher seats. It's fan friendly. When we started it, we pre-sold one hundred assigned seats. Now we're over one thousand pre-sold assigned seats."

Robinson points out that a coach can teach all the wrestling technique in the world, but the sport won't grow unless a fan base is developed. "Coaches need to get past the idea that a wrestling match is for Mom and Dad and the girlfriend to attend. It can and should be so much more than what it is. Too many coaches are just going through the motions, and the sport is suffering."

Each season the University of Minnesota wrestling team prints a team poster with an original theme. When people hang the poster, it serves as instant advertising. "We want a poster that grabs you. We want people to think it's so cool they want to hang it in their rooms. You need to spend time coming up with an idea. You can only make a first impression once."

The media can also be a good asset in promoting a program. It is a good idea to develop relationships with local print media as well as television and radio. It is helpful to know the names of the reporters who cover sports and to notify them of important matches or other human interest stories that pertain to your wrestlers.

"Coaches need to learn to feed the press. You need to help them come up with the story ideas. Don't sit around and wait for them to come to you; you have to go directly to them. You can even designate a person to give story suggestions to the media every week," said Robinson. "You can't wait for things to happen; you have to artificially create it. You have to sell this sport like you would sell underwear. You have to take your product to the people."

Robinson isn't only focused on his own team; he has concerns for wrestling in general.

"I really want to see this sport grow. Wrestling can be big. It has a uniqueness that no other sport has. When an athlete has to cut weight, he has to live it 24 hours a day. Wrestlers learn to produce consistently, even in adversity. You learn to produce no matter how you feel. Wrestlers are very individualistic, but they are team-oriented. These are developed life skills that everybody wants when they hire a person. These guys are high-functioning no matter how they feel."

Robinson thinks that wrestling offers the values that all families desire. Those values—discipline, sacrifice, and hard work—are what wrestling is all about.

"Wrestling is a great sport for kids because it teaches discipline and there is a place for everyone. Everyone wants to be great, but without a great effort. Wrestling disciplines a person to learn what great effort really means," he said.

While not all people can be champions, it is a good idea to surround oneself with the best. "You need to keep in check the people you are running around with. Different groups take you in different directions. Peer pressure is the greatest pressure," he said. "The buddy system works well when you are with quality people because they will draw you into their world. Good people help each other find a purpose in life, and when you find your purpose, you have happiness."

Coach J Robinson's Favorite Drill

Hard Drilling

"When it comes to drilling, my favorite thing is hard drilling. I like to do everything hard for 15 to 20 minutes where one guy is going at 80 percent doing as much as he can and if he doesn't do the moves right, then the other guy doesn't give it to him. The key here is that he's drilling in a tempo that he would wrestle in a competition. Most people drill slow and simple, but that doesn't equate to competitive wrestling.

"It's like being in the army when they have you target shooting at a bull's-eye. Then in Vietnam the training shifted to pop-up targets where you walk down a trail and have to hit the pop-up targets. That became more realistic. That equates to the real thing. That makes a difference.

"It's the same thing in wrestling. You have to drill at the same tempo that you wrestle at if you want it to make a difference."

9
Speaking of Wrestling

Dennis Hastert, Speaker of the U.S. House of Representatives

As Speaker of the House, Dennis Hastert is one of the most powerful men in the United States. His journey from the northern Illinois farm where he grew up to his office in Washington, D.C., where he is the government's third in command under President George W. Bush has been filled with years of hard work. Hastert gives credit to his experiences in wrestling for helping to shape his work ethic.

As hectic as Hastert's schedule always is, he feels so passionate about wrestling that he took the time to share his insights about a sport he believes gave him the skills and confidence to do great things in his life.

Hastert began wrestling in the mid-1950s when he entered high school. He was also a lineman on the football team.

"I learned a lot playing sports in high school. I loved that experience. By playing sports you can learn so many things you need in life that affect your people skills. It helped me in politics, business, teaching, and coaching. These are life skills that you take with you anywhere you go. The lessons I took with me are valuable because they helped me to achieve my goals. That's what you have to do," Hastert said.

When Hastert was a freshman at Oswego High School in Kendall County, Illinois, he met Coach Ken Pickerill, the athletic director who was also the coach for football, wrestling, and baseball. A teacher as well, Pickerill taught biology and physical education. Hastert credits Pickerill for making a great impact on his life. In 1959 and 1960, Hastert's junior and senior years, the Oswego Panthers football and wrestling teams went undefeated. This is quite an accomplishment

Dennis Hastert's colleagues elected him Speaker of the House, the third highest government office in the United States, in 1999. Hastert is now serving his 4th term as Speaker, and his 10th term as a Republican member of Congress representing Illinois' 14th Congressional District.

(Photo courtesy of Office of Congressman J. Dennis Hastert.)

considering Oswego was the smallest high school in the state. Hastert was named first-string tackle on the All-State team. As soon as Hastert hung up his cleats, he took out his wrestling shoes and headed for the mats, where he was the team's heavyweight at 190 pounds.

"First of all, I have to say I was not a great wrestler. I was an average athlete at a little country school, but I had a coach who took an interest in me and taught me that I could do things that I never even dreamed of doing," Hastert recalled. "That coach proved to a bunch of farm kids that we could really go out there and do things. That's the legacy of the sport. That's what gave me a lifelong love for the sport."

One reason Oswego become successful is that Pickerill set up matches with the biggest and best schools in the state because he felt that was the only way to improve. While Oswego High had about 300 total students, other schools from Joliet (about 4,000 students), Pekin, Oak Lawn, St. Charles, Libertyville, Lockport, and Naperville were much larger and provided tough competition.

"I recently went back to my old high school to see the team wrestle. I was happy to see that they can still go out there and be aggressive," he said.

After Hastert graduated from Oswego, he headed to Wheaton College in Wheaton, Illinois—a strict, conservative Christian school. He later earned a master's degree from Northern Illinois University. From there he became a high school teacher at Yorkville where he was the head wrestling coach and assistant football coach. His goal in wrestling was to keep it simple and teach the basics very well.

"Wrestling is an ancient sport. It goes back to biblical times. It is deep in the history of Mongolia, Korea, Mesopotamia, and Turkey and just about everywhere else. It has always been a natural thing for kids to do," Hastert said. "It's a competition that puts wrestlers out there and on their own and builds confidence."

Hastert not only built confidence in his young wrestlers, but he built a winning tradition as well. He had 82 athletes on his team at one time and had enough wrestlers to fill out freshman, sophomore, junior varsity, and varsity teams. He took many of his wrestlers on trips to attend clinics and camps. While traveling, Hastert, who was a history, government, and economics teacher, made stops at important historic sites to give lessons in American history.

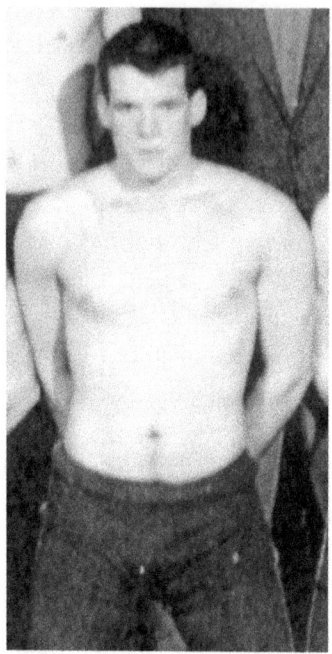

Dennis Hastert as a young wrestler at Oswego High School in Kendall County, Illinois.
(Photo courtesy of Office of Congressman J. Dennis Hastert.)

"When it came to coaching, one of the first things that I learned is that as much as I respected my old coach and the way he did things, I had to be myself and set my own goals. That's the advice I give coaches today. Don't try to be something or someone else. Just be yourself and make sure that you really like to work with kids. The ability to communicate with kids is the key to coaching," Hastert said.

Hastert believed in mixing hard work with fun when he coached. He had several basic principles he followed in his coaching that he still believes in today, including proper preparation, focus, discipline, and patience. Once you are properly prepared, you should never underestimate your opponent. Hastert believed in keeping the coaching within the wrestling room and not sitting in the coaches' corner shouting out instructions during match time. His basic advice to wrestlers is that when you are in a position to score, you better get the points on the scoreboard because the opportunity may not present itself again.

"I like to underpromise and overproduce," he said. As a coach, he never boasted about his teams. He let the results do the talking. In 1976 Yorkville won the Class A state title and Hastert was named Illinois Coach of the Year.

Parents play an important role in the life of a wrestler, and Hastert says that your child's participation in the sport is for his or her own benefit. "Win or lose, parents need to support their child. The biggest thing is that when they go out for a sport, they are making a commitment. Parents need to support the child to make sure they follow the rules and understand that the coach is volunteering to make the child a better person," Hastert explained. He added, "Everything comes down to commitment. That, right there, is a great life lesson. The child commits to the ideals of the sport. This is where he or she can prove that you can achieve anything in life if you're consistent and you work for it."

In 1980 Hastert decided to start practicing what he had been teaching for more than 16 years. He ran and won a seat as a state representative in the Illinois General Assembly. Although Hastert was accustomed to speaking in front of groups when he was teaching and coaching, he found that he got very nervous when he had to speak in a political arena. Then he decided that giving a speech is like wrestling in a match, if you practice consistently, you get better at it.

"Wrestling taught me determination and how not to give in to the little things. That's the same drive that is needed when I have to solve problems every day to keep the legislature and the country moving," he said.

He served six years in the Illinois legislature before being elected to the U.S. House of Representatives in 1986. He has also served as Chief Deputy Majority Whip, a leadership position he held for five years. In 1999, Hastert's colleagues elected him Speaker of the House, the third highest government official in the United States. Hastert is now serving his 4th term as Speaker and his 10th term as a Republican member of Congress representing Illinois' 14th Congressional District.

When Hastert became Speaker of the House, he chose some Abraham Lincoln memorabilia to accent the décor in his office. Since Lin-

coln and Hastert share an Illinois connection, Hastert believes Lincoln is a good representative of the Republican Party.

When asked if Lincoln is a good representative of wrestling, Hastert replied, "The old Jack Armstrong and Lincoln matches are legend. This reconfirms what I have always said about wrestling, that it has a cultural history in our country. The sport gives an opportunity for young men, and women now too, to go out, get in shape to compete, and be able to excel."

Although Hastert left teaching and coaching, his enthusiasm for wrestling has never diminished. He was inducted as an Outstanding American into the National Wrestling Hall of Fame in Stillwater, Oklahoma, in 2000. In 2001, the United States Olympic Committee named him Honorary Vice President of the American Olympic movement.

"Keeping wrestling alive in this country is very important. Those people who go out and coach and mentor do it because they want to help kids learn to help themselves. Wrestling took a bad rap for a while because people think it's WWF or whatever the fake wrestling on television is called. Wrestling is a good, wholesome sport. There are lots of opportunities for kids to get involved with wrestling through school teams and Beat the Streets programs. The sport is great because it cuts across economic and cultural lines," he said.

Wrestling is a team sport. While each match is an individual effort, the outcome of all the separate matches affects the team's overall score. "Everything you do, you help the team to win. There's no one to blame but yourself if you get pinned. Win or lose, though, it's you out there performing. You take the joy if you win, and you take the disappointment if you lose. That's the character-building part of the sport. It puts the responsibility on the individual, and there is no one to point the finger at but yourself," Hastert said.

While there are times when Hastert misses his coaching and teaching days, he enjoys his responsibilities in Washington, D.C. "Some days I do miss it, but I still have a lot of competition in my life," he said.

When Hastert is not in Washington, D.C., he lives in Yorkville, Illinois, along the Fox River with his wife, Jean. They have two grown sons, Ethan and Joshua. Whenever he can find free time, he enjoys attending wrestling meets, fishing, restoring vintage automobiles, and carving and painting duck decoys.

10
Pioneer in Women's Wrestling

Tricia Saunders, World Champion Wrestler

The only thing Tricia Saunders wanted to do as a youngster in Michigan was to wrestle. It never occurred to her that ponytails and takedowns don't mix. She immersed herself in an arena where girls rarely appeared to work out and compete. At nine years old and 45 pounds, Saunders entered her first wrestling tournament in 1974 because she wanted to pursue what she loved. She won most of her matches in that tournament, and what happened there set the stage for her career.

Tricia Saunders has her arm raised in another victory for U.S. Olympic women's wrestling.
(Photo courtesy of USA Wrestling.)

"People didn't react well to me being in that tournament. They told me I should go home because I shouldn't be there," Saunders said. "Then there were other people who thought it was all about women's liberation. This was back in the time of Billie Jean King and Bobby Riggs, and people started telling me that I was doing a great thing for women's liberation. I didn't understand what they were talking about. I am all about the sport, but my biggest legacy is what I did for women. I wanted wrestling for everyone. I really did just like to wrestle."

Saunders grew up in a wrestling family in Ann Arbor, Michigan. Her brothers were wrestlers, and her father coached the club team. She went along to the practices and stayed on the sidelines in the beginning, but it didn't take long before she was learning the moves and wrestling with the boys. She was accepted in the room because everyone knew her and her family. It was the rest of society that became uncomfortable with the idea of a girl wrestling.

"I grew up in an intellectual university town so the concept of a girl wrestling with boys was okay. The club I was in had great lead-

ers who accepted me. I knew everyone in the room because of my father, and my older brother was a state champ. It only became difficult when I went to tournaments and other people gave me all kinds of grief," she explained.

Saunders pulled energy from those negative reactions to become an advocate for the development of women's wrestling. There were no opportunities available for her to wrestle in high school, so she pursued gymnastics and baseball, her other athletic interests. Then, in the late 1980s, when women's wrestling became an international sport, she went back to wrestling and had so much success that she is now considered the greatest women's wrestler in American history.

Saunders is a four-time World Champion (1992, 1996, 1998, and 1999) and the 1993 World silver medalist. She won 11 national titles. She served as a U.S. Olympic coach for the first women's team at the 2004 Olympics in Athens. She is the first woman inducted as a Distinguished Member of the National Wrestling Hall of Fame in the 30th anniversary class of 2006. When she retired in 2001, she had never lost a single match to a U.S. competitor in women's wrestling.

"I am proud of being inducted into the Wrestling Hall of Fame. I think it is amazing being in that kind of company. When I was growing up, all of my idols were men. I do have to admit, though, that I feel awkward getting in there ahead of some of the men who are also deserving. I feel proud of my medals and accomplishments as an athlete," Saunders said.

Saunders loved to compete and having the opportunity to do so on an international level was a highlight in her career.

"Competing in the Worlds was great competition. It made me feel that everything I did in the sport was worth it. There is no greater feeling than to stand on the podium and hear our national anthem being played. International competition is a fantastic experience. I loved seeing all the flags and the delegates from the different countries. It is nice to walk up and shake hands with women from all over the world. If it weren't for the international competitions, I never would have met so many dynamic people," she said.

By the time the United States had a women's Olympic wrestling team, Saunders was past her competing days. However, she and her husband, Townsend Saunders, who won a silver medal in the 1996 Olympics, joined Coach Terry Steiner in training the women's 2004 Olympic team. That team won silver and bronze medals.

The road to glory and pushing for women's opportunities within wrestling had its share of bumps for Saunders. At age 23, Saunders was trying to make changes and was waiting for the politics within the sport to swing in her favor. From the earliest days of adults not accepting her presence in the boys' tournaments right up through her serving in many leadership positions within USA Wrestling, Saunders met with resistance.

"I realized early on that I was going to take some heat from people. I knew I had to be a thorn in people's sides. I was tired of people being polite to my face and agreeing with me, and then when a vote took place it would turn out 23–1 against me. It was disappointing to see people who said they would help make a change and then they weren't there for me. I remember being in tears in my sponsor's office. He said he'd kick the door open for me, but I was the one who had to go through that door. It was a pivotal moment. He told me that I wasn't going to make friends. I started researching laws and going about making changes that way," Saunders said.

Saunders was serving on decision-making boards within USA Wrestling at the same time that she was training for competition and starting her family. She has three children now. Amazingly, having babies didn't slow Saunders down or knock her out of her training regimen for too long. She brought her nine-month-old baby to the

Tricia Saunders is a pioneer in women's wrestling in the United States.
(Photo courtesy of USA Wrestling.)

1996 Worlds in Bulgaria because she was still nursing and refused to let her involvement with the sport get in the way of what she felt was best for her child.

"That was a rough trip. We had changed time zones, but the baby was still on her schedule so I was not getting any sleep at all. She was already walking at nine months, and she was a busy baby. I can remember warming up for a match pushing a stroller around, hoping she would fall asleep," Saunders recalled lightheartedly. "Now that's something the men wrestlers don't have to deal with."

When she was training at the Olympic center, she found that children were an unwelcome sight because they could be a distraction to the athletes. She had to eat her meals away from the team and the training center because children were not allowed in.

"I would like to see someday that there is an affiliate day-care center for people who train at the Olympic level. When you become the primary caretaker for a baby, your whole world changes and not everyone understands that. I always needed to solve problems. But that's what wrestling is, problem after problem that has to be solved. Every opponent is a problem that you have to solve," she said.

Saunders's efforts were recognized when she was awarded the first-ever USA Wrestling Woman of the Year Award in 1997. She was also the USA Wrestling Women's Wrestler of the Year twice and the United States Olympic Committee (USOC) Women's Wrestler of the Year three times. She served as the head coach for the U.S. women's team that competed in the 2003 Pan American Games, the first to include women's wrestling in the program. The United States swept all four gold medals in that event.

Saunders used her ability to persevere to earn a physician's assistant degree from Midwestern University. She spent 40 hours a week in class and studying and graduated with the highest honors, all while being a mom and an athlete in training.

"So many people told me that I couldn't do it because the course load was too demanding. If I learned anything from wrestling, it is that there is a way to get from point A to point B. Nothing comes easily. I felt very proud when I graduated summa cum laude. I couldn't make it to study groups or do the campaigning for good rotations. I was cutting weight and training and studying. I was always the last one out when I took a test because I made myself sit there and recheck every question. The people in my class were shocked when they

saw I had the highest honors. They didn't know that I had just won the Nationals at the same time either. No one knew the level that I was at," she said.

Saunders attributes her experiences with wrestling to building the confidence base that enables her to set goals and achieve them.

"I don't know if I could have done any of this without wrestling in my life. Wrestling gave me the confidence and having confidence in yourself is a huge gift. Wrestling taught me that you can create something out of nothing. Hard work pays off," she said.

Although the Saunderses both have made history in wrestling, it is not what their marriage revolves around. They met each other through wrestling, but they found that they had much more in common than just the sport.

"We were both very motivated in wrestling, and we have always understood each other's commitments to the sport. We both understand what it takes to get the job done, and we have a mutual respect. We have always had a great relationship outside of wrestling. Wrestling is not what our relationship is all about. There is so much more to us than wrestling," she explained.

They are also careful about not forcing their children into the sport. They have introduced wrestling to their children through the club team in their town, but they are introducing them to other sports as well.

"You can introduce wrestling to a child, but it takes a certain type of person to do it. It's a full combat sport. Only certain types of people like that. The wins and losses are so crystal clear, too, and that can be tough on a kid. It's not a sport that you can force on a person. They have to want to do it," she said.

Just like Saunders wanted to do it. As she has proven time and time again, when she wants to do something, she will find a way to get it done.

"People never saw me as an athlete alone. I was always considered to be an activist, too. There was a lot of grunt work that I had to do to help women's wrestling, but that's not necessarily the glory I want to be remembered for," she said.

What she will be remembered for is being a pioneer in U.S. women's wrestling history.

11
Role of the Assistant Coach

Assistant Coach Jim Heffernan, University of Illinois
Assistant Coaches Donny Pritzlaff and
Rob Anspach, Hofstra University

There is no one who knows the role of the assistant coach better than Jim Heffernan at the University of Illinois. At the start of his 14th season with the Fighting Illini where he is the assistant coach to Head Coach Mark Johnson, Heffernan shared some of his insights regarding the role of assistant that he has played for the past 17 years.

"As the assistant coach, I am involved in every aspect of the program, but the only drawback is that I am not the ultimate decision maker. I grew up in the Midwest so I love being here and my family is happy here," he said.

His family's happiness and the fact that wrestling is important to the University of Illinois athletic department is what keeps Heffernan content in his role. If that were not the case then he would probably be searching for a head coaching position.

"I would like to be a head coach, but I really like what I am doing here. I think that one huge advantage to being an assistant coach is that I can have a closer relationship to the wrestlers. I don't have to be the ultimate disciplinarian. I can get pretty close to the guys. I would say that I am the middleman, and I like it that way," he said.

It's fortunate for Illinois wrestling that Heffernan enjoys his role because he has the qualifications to be a head coach for any top program. Heffernan was a four-time All-American at the University of Iowa where he graduated in 1987. He was a member of three Hawkeye NCAA championships and four Big 10 championship teams. Heffernan was the Hawkeye captain during his senior year, and he was Iowa's Male Athlete of the Year in 1987. He started his coaching career as a graduate assistant at the University of Iowa before becoming an assistant coach at Lehigh University in 1988. He moved on to

Jim Heffernan has helped the University of Illinois program as assistant coach for 14 seasons.
(Photo courtesy of University of Illinois Sports Information Department.)

Oregon State in 1990 where he coached for two years with Johnson. He joined the Fighting Illini staff in 1992.

When Heffernan was a student at Iowa, Mark Johnson was working as an assistant coach at Iowa. The two seem to be following each other ever since. Heffernan credits their coaching success to their ability to work well together.

"When it comes to how to run a program, our basic philosophy is the same. Our working relationship is very good, which is very important. I've seen a lot of programs with a lot of infighting, which just doesn't work. My job is to enhance what the head coach is doing," he said.

Heffernan found it shocking when he left Iowa and started working for other programs. He discovered that the University of Iowa does not represent the real world of wrestling because the school gives the team a budget and a full staff and there are lots of fans. Not all schools are that supportive of their wrestling programs.

"When I was in Oregon, it was two hours before our first home meet and the gym was not set up. Some more time went by and it still was not set up yet. I kept wondering when it was going to be set up. Before long we realized it wasn't going to happen, so we went and rolled out the mats ourselves and set up the chairs and everything else. I learned to make a lot of adjustments, and it takes a lot of planning," he said.

Heffernan has been working with Johnson for so long that they complement each other. One coach's strengths are the other coach's weaknesses, so they have learned to coordinate their efforts. Neither coach has to tell the other one what to do, how to do it, or when to get it done because they move like clockwork.

"I tell people who want to pursue a career in coaching that you have to have a plan. You have to know what type of school you want to work at and where you want to live. Once you get there, then you have to surround yourself with good people," he said.

One of Heffernan's roles is to be there for the wrestlers off the mat and behind the scenes. He believes he is able to maintain a close relationship with the wrestlers by showing them that he cares. "I keep close tabs on them. We address things right away. We're not going to put up with anything too fragile. We're not going to let anyone pull us down. When you're dealing with 18- to 22-year-olds, they can sometimes find the wrong things to get into. These kids still need supervision and that's part of my job. I have to be an influence on

them and talk to them about the type of person they need to be on and off the mat," he said.

Heffernan deals with the wrestlers as individuals. He strives to be fair, consistent, and truthful, which he feels goes a long way in getting the team to believe in what the program is trying to accomplish.

"I think it is important to be clear with your expectations and goals for the group and to be flexible enough to adapt to the group you are working with. You really have to deal with each athlete individually," he said.

A key factor that is stressed at Illinois is academics. Although wrestling is a high priority, the academic side of student-athlete is the first concern. "You have to emphasize to the team that when you do better in school it will translate to other parts of your life that are important to you. As a sport, wrestling represents what is right in college athletics. Wrestlers don't have the million dollar contracts waiting for them. It is not difficult to sell the message that you have to go to school, work hard, earn your degree, and move on," he said.

Heffernan enjoys the life lessons that wrestling teaches a person. He finds it intriguing to watch wrestlers come in as kids and transform into adults before they graduate. "The sport teaches good principles for life. It teaches strong work habits, discipline and toughness, accountability, and setting and achieving goals. Nothing is ever given to you in wrestling because everything has to be earned. The sport is a lot like making a living, without the benefits of earning a paycheck.

"There are times when wrestling is hard. You don't want to practice, you don't want to have to put in extra time, you don't want to have to make weight and run the extra mile. Wrestling teaches that if you don't do the extra things, then you don't separate yourself from anyone. Wrestling is a long set of life skills classes that are difficult to pass, but once you have, then nothing else is difficult. As an assistant coach, I am there to help out with all of those details," he said.

Hofstra's 2006 Assistant Coaches

During the 2006 season Hofstra University had a pair of dynamic assistant coaches with Rob Anspach and Donny Pritzlaff. Anspach,

Role of the Assistant Coach

who wrestled for Hofstra under Coach Tom Ryan, was happy to contribute as a coach to the program.

"I coached Rob and really got to know him. He is intelligent, hard-working, and well grounded. Those are all attributes to look for in an assistant coach. He is an outstanding coach and he has a passion for wrestling," Ryan said.

Pritzlaff, a two-time NCAA champion and four-time All-American at the University of Wisconsin, is combining coaching with his own personal training for the 2008 Olympics. Ryan actively recruited Pritzlaff because he knew he would be great for the Hofstra program.

"I loved being at Hofstra. It was close to home [New Jersey], and I got to work with wrestlers on the East Coast. As an assistant coach I provided some stability to the program. I think it's important to have a coach that can work out with the team, and I'd say that's my best attribute. You can always watch a wrestler and pick things up, but for me, I can wrestle with them and actually feel their mistakes. I can feel where their flaws are. That's the best way to make them better," Pritzlaff said.

The fact that Ryan, Anspach, and Pritzlaff are all friends added an element of harmony to the program.

Donny Pritzlaff combined coaching at Hofstra University with training for the Olympics.
(Photo courtesy of Bruce Curtis.)

"I always liked being in wrestling so when this opportunity came, it was perfect. I couldn't be happier. I'm involved in every aspect of the program from recruiting to training and daily workouts," Anspach said.

During the 2006 season, the Hofstra coaching staff took a divided approach to its team as each coach had full responsibility for seven wrestlers. With 21 wrestlers in the program, the staff found it could micromanage the team and give each wrestler personal attention. While the coaches had their own seven wrestlers to focus on, they naturally crossed over to all of the wrestlers during workouts.

"We were assigned certain wrestlers and were responsible for all aspects of their college life. There was a lot of pressure for us to get our guys to perform. They are here to get a college education and a degree so we had to monitor their academics. We monitored their weight control, their workouts, extra technique sessions, and many other things. We had to be regimented because some of them are only 18 years old and this is the first time that they are on their own. We had to help them along and get them ready to wrestle. It was all about the team getting better," Anspach said.

While the team was split into three mini-groups, Hofstra still functioned as a whole team and did a lot together as a group. The sense of team was always at the forefront.

One important coaching philosophy held in high regard was personal accountability—both for the coaches and the wrestlers. "We were big on accountability. We held ourselves accountable for every little detail, and we told our wrestlers that they had to be accountable for themselves. Holding yourself accountable takes you way past wrestling and into life. If you learn anything from wrestling, it's that you have to always think about what you're doing and that your actions have some consequences," Anspach said.

At Hofstra and now at Ohio State, Ryan takes personal responsibility for the development of his assistant coaches. "I feel it is important to keep the assistant coaches fully involved. You never know, if something ever happens to me, they're ready for the job," he said.

One major role the assistant coaches are involved in is recruiting. There is a lot of focus on attracting the right wrestler to fit with the philosophy of the program. Some of the features the coaches look for in high school wrestlers are how aggressively they wrestle, how fine-tuned their technique is, what their work ethic is, and what their overall character is like. The coaches also like to spend time talking with the family of the potential recruit.

"We have to make sure the wrestler fits in with our overall plan. Recruiting the right wrestler is crucial because once he is in the program, he affects everyone on the team. We're not looking to make them mini-versions of our wrestling style, but we take what they know and direct them to keep learning," Anspach said.

The coaching staff plans carefully who they are interested in recruiting and when they are going to see the wrestlers in competition. NCAA regulations allow coaches to see recruits four times, so their goal is to watch them wrestle in challenging matches.

"I enjoy the recruiting part of coaching. As coaches we want to see how they are currently wrestling in competitive matches. It's a tough call sometimes because you're never really sure how good a wrestler can be until you get him into your room. Some people are late bloomers and some are already men in ninth grade. Some wrestlers look mediocre in high school, and then they are unbelievable in college," Anspach said.

Not only was each coach responsible for his seven wrestlers and recruiting duties, they had other job duties as well. For example, Anspach handled the travel arrangements with booking flights, buses, and hotels, while Pritzlaff managed the recruiting strategies. Organization is the key to keeping a program running correctly.

"I had all the travel arrangements set in September before the season even started. I had files and folders and tried to stay very organized. Naturally, unexpected things can come up, but I found that being organized helped to keep it all under control," Anspach said.

Communication between the three coaches is what helped to maintain harmony within the program.

"The biggest thing we did was speak up and say what we thought. We did it behind closed doors so that it gives the head coach time to take everything into consideration. He [Ryan] respected our opinions, but he ultimately made the decisions. I've been around wrestling for a long time as well, so I was comfortable adding my perspective. We were all on the same page and together on the decisions that were made. Once a decision was made, then we were one voice and we moved forward from there," Anspach said.

12
Surrounding Yourself with Good People

Ben Peterson, Olympic Gold Medalist

If Ben Peterson wasn't blessed with a supportive family, he might never have taken the path that led to Olympic gold. When Peterson wrestled during his high school freshman season, he had seven matches and lost all of them. The truth is he was pinned in all seven matches. Some families might have given up right then, but the Petersons weren't about to give up.

"My family had high expectations and helped me set high goals for myself. They encouraged me to strive for those goals that I didn't initially see that I was fit for. I am glad and very

proud that I met those goals. I really don't know where I'd be without my family," Peterson said.

Peterson, who is a deeply spiritual man, acknowledges that the success in his life stems from his deep faith, his hard work, and the great people surrounding him.

"I am thankful for the people that God has seen fit to put me in touch with," he said.

One of six children, Peterson grew up in the small Wisconsin town of Comstock, the son of a dairy farmer. He and four brothers all played football and wrestled at nearby Cumberland High School. Little in his early years of wrestling indicated he had the ability to win a major college scholarship, much less national championships and Olympic medals. When Peterson first tried the sport after his three older brothers wrestled, he admits his early days were not the brightest.

"A key individual at that point in my life was my brother Phil. He was playing football at the University of Wisconsin. When he came home, he taught me how to lift and train at a time when no one was doing that kind of training. He later was drafted into the army, and he kept sending me letters of encouragement," Peterson explained.

Phil helped to train Ben during the summer before Ben's senior year in high school. All of the training paid off as Ben went undefeated during the regular season that year. On the second day of the state tournament, Ben was surprised by his brother's attendance at the competition because it was a long haul from Kentucky for a weekend leave. But Ben was thrilled his brother had made it in time for the finals where he faced Rich Heinbaugh from Monroe, Wisconsin. As Ben recalls, the first period was scoreless and the second period started with Ben in the bottom position. He escaped easily.

"I was surprised how easily I got out, and then I thought, why not go for a reversal and get two points instead of one. So I used a wizzer to step over him, and within seconds I was on my back fighting frantically," he recalled.

Peterson was stunned as his opponent pinned him in the finals. All he wanted to do was to get out of the gym. Phil, who was crying, came to his side. The memory of that moment has returned many times over the years in Ben's mind, and the last thing he ever wanted to do was to disappoint his big brother, his hero, ever again. He recommitted himself and worked even harder.

Ben Peterson lectures wrestlers at his camp called Camp of Champs, which he runs with his brother John, also an Olympic gold medalist.
(Photo courtesy of Ben Peterson.)

While he didn't win any Wisconsin state championships, Peterson did show enough promise that his high school coach took him to the Olympic trials at Ames, Iowa, in 1968. He was eliminated from the tournament quickly with a pin and a 12–3 loss in two matches.

"I had the tar beat out of me in two matches. I had to go against a new recruit for Iowa State. I had one takedown and put him on his back, and then he just thrashed me," Peterson said.

All was not lost, however, as Harold Nichols, the coach at Iowa State, was there and saw something that he liked in Ben, offering him a partial scholarship.

"He was a shrewd and discerning businessman. He was strong and intense. He set a stage that was valuable to me," Peterson said of Nichols.

The stage that was set is considered the glory years for the Iowa State Cyclones. It was the era of wrestlers Dan Gable, Chuck Jean, Jason Smith, Dale Bahr, Dave Martin, Carl Adams, and Chris Taylor in the late 1960s and early 1970s. In 1969, when Peterson was a fresh-

man, the Cyclones had nine All-Americans and won the first of three NCAA wrestling team titles in a four-year stretch.

"I knew about Dan Gable, but I didn't know how extraordinary he was. He trained nonstop. Here was this scrawny guy that I outweighed by 50 pounds, and he was whipping me," Peterson said.

Peterson benefited from Gable's influence, setting his sights on being an NCAA champion, which he achieved in 1971 and 1972 at 190 pounds. His success didn't stop there as he captured the Olympic gold medal in freestyle wrestling in 1972 and then the silver medal in 1976. In the boycott year of 1980, Peterson became only the fourth American wrestler to make three Olympic teams.

Interestingly, his brother John, one year older than Ben, gained international acclaim after wrestling at University of Wisconsin-Stout. John was a silver medalist the year Ben won his Olympic gold medal, and then they switched in 1976 with John winning and Ben placing second.

"When I was a senior at Iowa, my brother John came over to work out with me and Gable. The three of us had round-robin wrestling

Ben Peterson celebrates another victory on his way to capturing the Olympic gold medal in freestyle in 1972 and then the silver medal in 1976. In the U.S. Olympic boycott year of 1980, he became only the fourth American wrestler to make three Olympic teams.
(Photo courtesy of Ben Peterson.)

tournaments. I would love to watch those matches today because they were wild. I watched John and Gable go at it, and I realized that I had to get in there with them," he said. "It was those two that gave me the idea to go for the Olympics."

After he made the 1972 Olympic team, nobody thought Peterson would do much because college wrestlers don't readily adapt to the differences in international freestyle competition. He was working out with his brother and with Gable three to five times a week in freestyle.

"John and I soaked up everything that Gable gave us. He kept telling us that we could beat these guys and that we could win at the Olympics. That meant a lot because other people in the country were wondering what we thought we were doing," he said.

Peterson stunned spectators by pinning Roussi Petrov, Bulgaria's world champion, in the semifinals. That's what won the gold medal for him, because he had one more pin than Soviet Ennado Strakhov, which determined the final placing after they fought to a 2–2 draw.

The Petersons wanted the best for their children. His father only went to school for seven years before he started working full-time on the dairy farm, and his mother had a high school education.

"When we were growing up, my parents talked to us about *when* we would go to college. It was never *if* we would go to college," Peterson said.

Ironically, Mrs. Peterson was initially opposed to the idea of her boys wrestling. She saw glimpses of the fake wrestling on television and thought that's what the sport was all about.

"She only knew the gross and vulgar wrestling of professional wrestling. She wouldn't even sign the form for my older brother to wrestle. My dad took it and signed it and said it would be okay. My mother eventually started going to matches, and she became a great promoter of wrestling. People would ask her what it's like to be the mother of two Olympic champions. She would respond by telling other people that whatever you do, you have to let your boys wrestle," he recalled.

Once Mrs. Peterson overcame her first impressions of the sport, she became 100 percent supportive of her sons.

"Many kids today don't have that beginning encouragement. After John and I won the two Olympics we decided to start a wrestling camp," he said.

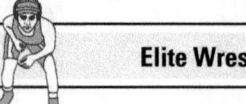

Camp of Champs began in 1977 and currently draws more than five hundred wrestlers to its summer program at Camp Forest Springs in the North Woods of Wisconsin. Not only does Peterson bring his Olympic and collegiate successes to the campers, but he also draws from the 27 seasons he spent as head wrestling coach at Maranatha Baptist Bible College in Watertown. The camp is a combination of wrestling, Bible study, and recreation. When Peterson is not coordinating details of his camps, he also does a great deal of traveling around the country to give motivational speeches.

"When I talk to groups of wrestlers, I talk about working hard and using your God-given talents so that you have enjoyable memories. In our camp setting, we have an interesting perspective on how we approach the kids. We have a gracious, nonpushy way about how we talk about God. Our wrestlers are from every church denomination there is. Many campers don't have knowledge of God's word, and campers thank us for how gentle we are about it. I talk to them about my desire to thank God for giving me talent and ability. That has always been a key motivator for me," Peterson explained.

Peterson feels that wrestlers who learn to develop a deeper understanding of their faith oftentimes improve on the wrestling mat as well. He shares this message when he travels. At the Midlands Tournament, he gave a clinic and then invited the wrestlers to the chapel where he gave one of his testimonials.

"You need to build your faith as much as you build yourself physically for competition," he said. "Wrestling is difficult and demanding, and it stretches you more than any other sport. There's uniqueness to wrestling. It strains a person in so many ways. It is so much like life. It teaches you to keep your hope up. It is not always fun, but it can be very rewarding."

13
Peaking Throughout the Season and the Essence of Speed

Coach Carl Adams,
Boston University

The wrestling season is a long process. Boston University coach Carl Adams recognizes that there are many times throughout the season when a wrestler needs to bring together the mental and physical aspects of the sport. This is known as *peaking*.

"The end of the season is the point when your conditioning, technique, nutrition, and mental preparation must come together and be at the highest possible level. If a wrestler can

get these four things at a premium, then the performance will be at a premium, too," he said.

Adams notes that all wrestlers need to find the right balance of good nutrition, mental alertness, and overall physical well-being before the season even starts. An athlete needs as much energy, both physically and mentally, and it starts with how you fuel your body. It is worth consulting with a nutrition expert to follow a prescribed plan of action throughout the season. Not all foods are created equal, and it is a good idea to pay close attention to how food affects each individual wrestler. It is not an easy process to find the right balance.

"I like to think of it as a gardening process. You get the soil ready and plant the seeds. The more you take care of it in each phase, the more food you will get out of the garden when it finally produces. That's what peaking is all about," he explained.

Adams has seen enough wrestling in 40 years to know what it takes for a wrestler to pull it all together and be at his best when it really counts. Adams learned from personal experience as he was a two-time NCAA champion at 158 pounds for Iowa State in 1971 and 1972. He was a three-time All American, and he was on three NCAA championship teams for Iowa State.

Adams continued his wrestling career after Iowa, capturing the National AAU Freestyle Championships in 1973 and 1975. He fol-

Boston University coach Carl Adams encourages one of his wrestlers during a match.
(Photo courtesy of Boston University Sports Information Department.)

lowed with a silver medal at the Pan American Games and a third-place showing in the World Championships, both in 1975.

"I have witnessed wrestlers with a losing record go on to win the NCAA tournament. I have seen some wrestlers do a miraculous turnaround in a season. I have seen backup wrestlers and nonstarters be inserted into the starting lineup to go on to win state and national titles. We knew that each of these wrestlers had it in them," he said.

What needs to happen for a wrestler to be at his best when it will mean the most?

Adams believes there are a few simple measures a wrestler can take. First, it is important to understand that the healthier a person is, the better the performance will be. A wrestler needs to minimize his chances of getting injured.

"The key is to guard against injuries in the practice room. Be careful of working out with unfamiliar workout partners from other programs. This is often a major hazard," he said. "Don't let pride and ego get in the way of what you are trying to accomplish in your workout. When you need to peak, stay with familiar partners who will push you."

He also noted that it is a good idea to avoid wrestling someone who is not near your weight class. Wrestling someone heavier is potentially dangerous.

Along with the nutritional focus, a wrestler needs to make weight. "You should not be cutting more than a couple of pounds the day before you have to step on the scale. You should plan your weight-making routine so that you can have a good meal the night before and something else to eat on the day you have to step on the scale. You will find that you have much more energy and a higher level of concentration if you do this," he said.

Another component to peaking at the right times is rest, which is crucial in recovering from difficult workouts. Some of the greatest deterrents of getting adequate rest are television, computer, video games, and pointless "hanging out." Wrestlers need to discipline themselves to build rest into their daily routine.

In addition, a wrestler should focus on major conditioning six weeks prior to the competitions at the end of the season. Adams suggests that adding another small layer of physical conditioning with less than two or three weeks remaining in the season is beneficial. He suggests that running long distance, doing extra sprints, and wrestling hard will enhance a wrestler's condition. Keep in mind that

you have to know when to back off, too. There will be a point at which you will get diminishing results from overworking yourself.

"Typically, you should back off a couple of days before you compete. You need to let your body rest at a certain point because you are not helping your cause by draining the energy that you need to compete with," Adams said.

The mind is a powerful thing. A wrestler's mind-set and mental preparation is the driving force behind success. In order to flip the mental switch on, you have to believe that your potential to achieve is virtually unlimited.

"You have to believe and come to the realization that you have the ability to unleash your potential at any time. All you have to do is believe, believe, and believe," Adams stressed. "Your mind-set and your thought process is the engine that drives everything you do physically. You need to get the physical and mental side of wrestling to melt into one."

In order to achieve this physical and mental convergence, each wrestler should set a clear goal for himself and make an unwavering commitment to that goal.

"Your goal must become a part of who you are and what you want to achieve. You need to visualize and feel your goal happening on a daily basis," Adams said.

Adams suggests daily routines that will help wrestlers achieve their goals. Start by writing your goal on a piece of paper and placing it in an area so that you can see it as often as possible throughout the day. Hang it on your bedroom door or write it on the cover of your favorite notebook or agenda. Say your goal privately to yourself as many times as possible throughout the day. These are ways to help make your goal part of your subconscious and your conscious thought process.

Adams knows the benefits of using mental imagery in wrestling, which is a powerful tool. Anytime you have a quiet moment to yourself, get into a totally relaxed state both physically and mentally. Close your eyes and try to visualize yourself competing against the individuals you will have to defeat. Try to visualize every aspect of what will happen in your competition. Picture yourself warming up for the match, sense the smell of the mat, and watch yourself walk out to shake hands with the opponent. Visualize yourself wrestling and scoring points . . . winning all scramble situations . . . not giving an

inch on any physical or mental battles . . . reacting swiftly to all situations and attacking every opening . . . completely surprising your opponent and breaking his spirit . . . tirelessly pursuing the opposition . . . proudly having your hand raised in victory!

The Essence of Speed

Speed is an important factor that helps define athletic greatness and can often be the deciding factor when it comes to winning or losing in any athletic event. Speed can be the trump card for those who have it, and it can be a terrible menace for those who have to compete against it. It is an asset that a coach looks for when building a team, and an attribute that athletes seek to improve through training.

"Speed is an asset that I look for when I recruit, and an advantage that I push my wrestlers to acquire more of when they train," said Adams. "I had many people tell me that I used to be one of those quick wrestlers. When you have speed, you know you have a special gift that you can use whenever you need it."

Boston University coach Carl Adams stresses to his athletes the importance of peaking by the end of the season.
(Photo courtesy of Carl Adams.)

A wrestler needs to recognize the importance of speed and also needs to work on improving speed from every position every day of practice. Adams feels that there are four different speed categories for wrestlers: slow, average, fast, and superfast. Fast wrestlers have the ability to be champions at any level. Wrestlers who fall into the slow category have difficulty competing against top-level wrestlers. All wrestlers have the ability to improve upon speed.

The six concepts that Adams knows will improve a wrestler's speed are position, timing, anticipation, power, coordination, and precision technique. Here's how Adams instructs his wrestlers about each of these concepts.

1. **Position:** "Knowing how to stay in good position is the key to being a good wrestler because it enables you to attack and defend efficiently. When you wrestle in the neutral position you should be as close as possible to the target before attacking. Analyzing various wrestling positions, setups, and wrestling skills will be the most productive time wrestlers can spend learning how to become better competitors."
2. **Timing:** "Good timing can increase your speed dramatically. It generally relates to the setup, moving on the whistle, and how well you are able to anticipate. If a takedown setup causes an opponent to expose a weakness while you are moving toward him, then your speed automatically improves because you have two forces moving toward each other. Good timing and quick reactions allow a wrestler to attack the weakness before the opportunity closes."
3. **Anticipation:** "Cael Sanderson is the best at anticipating the movement of an opponent and attacking the exposed weakness. It seems as though he has a sixth sense when it comes to anticipating how and where an opponent's next move will be. Wrestlers should experiment in practice how an opponent will react to various setups. Choreographed drilling is also a great way to improve how well you anticipate. Your speed can improve considerably as you expand your ability to anticipate."
4. **Power:** "Weight training will improve your power and power will improve your speed. Most athletes look for ways to improve their strength and explosive power. The key with strength training is to target specific muscle groups that wrestlers rely on when they attack and defend."

5. **Coordination:** "Coordination has a lot to do with refining technique and constantly improving efficiency. I have seen many wrestlers chop the takedown setup, level change, and penetration step into three different parts when they execute it. This can really slow down the attack. The most efficient way to execute the takedown is to blend those individual components all into one effort. You need to make sure you don't telegraph your intentions because that will slow you down as well. Eliminating hitches and extra movement is another way to refine technique and improve quickness."

6. **Precision Technique:** "It is worth every bit of effort to learn and refine skills. The more refined your skills are, the quicker you will be. Good technical wrestlers waste a lot less energy and can better exploit an opponent's weaknesses."

A combination of speed with the element of surprise makes for a tough wrestler. Adams tells his wrestlers that they are training to be great.

"There's too much work that goes into wrestling to be average. Great athletes train to be the best that they can be. It's a very individual thing," he said.

14
Wrestling Leads to Nobel Peace Prize

*Dr. Norman Borlaug,
1970 Nobel Peace Prize Winner*

No one could have predicted that the lessons learned on a wrestling mat could spark the drive to solve world hunger. But that's just what happened when revolutionary scientist Dr. Norman Borlaug stepped on the mat to begin his life's training. It all began in the extreme northeast corner of Iowa back in the early 1930s. Drilling technique and working through a tough conditioning regimen garnered the discipline it would take to later lead the Green Revolution of the Third World in the 1960s.

Dr. Norman Borlaug won the Nobel Peace Prize in 1970.
(Photo courtesy of Dr. Norman Borlaug.)

That was when Dr. Borlaug performed miracles with grain and saved millions of people from starvation. His fight to solve world hunger was recognized when he won the 1970 Nobel Peace Prize.

Now in his early nineties, Dr. Borlaug is still creating angles on how to take down hunger in deprived nations. He has no intentions of ending his campaign until there are no starving people left in this world. His current conditioning regimen is walking through plagued fields in Africa, Argentina, Pakistan, India, and other countries where he analyzes crops to help find solutions to diseases and poor agricultural conditions.

Dr. Borlaug, who speaks with the mental sharpness of a man much younger than his age, says wrestling is where it all began. "I spent 61 years in Third World agriculture, and a lot of those years I lived outside of the United States working on food production problems. When you deal with the hungry nations in this world, there can be some pretty dark situations. It was in those dark times when I found myself reflecting back on my wrestling days. Wrestling gave me the courage to get the technology to help develop the crops and the courage to keep moving forward," Dr. Borlaug said.

The courage and discipline Dr. Borlaug developed in his wrestling career started in his high school days in Cresco, Iowa, where the principal, David Bartelma, also served as the wrestling coach. He was a tough disciplinarian.

"I garnered a lot from him. He told us that we had to give our best or don't bother to come out because it would be a waste of time for the rest of the team," Dr. Borlaug said. He learned to compete, making it to the state finals in 1932. He remained out of school during the worst of the Depression, finally enrolling at the University of Minnesota in the fall of 1933 where he wrestled at 145 pounds and studied forestry.

When the University of Minnesota coach retired, Dr. Borlaug lobbied to have his high school coach hired to fill the vacancy. Coach Bartelma not only led the Minnesota team, but he organized wrestling clinics for high school football coaches to attract future wrestlers throughout the state. He sent Dr. Borlaug, who by then had success in the Big 10 tournament, and other members of the team to put on wrestling exhibitions to help promote the sport in Minnesota.

"He used to put us on a bus and give us 25 cents for meal money to go around the state to show wrestling to parents, teachers, and coaches. I saw high school wrestling catch on in Minnesota," Dr. Borlaug said.

During the 2005 season he watched a duel match between Iowa and Minnesota that was attended by thirteen thousand people. "When we started wrestling in Minnesota, there were only a handful of people. The rules and regulations are different now, but the basic principles of the sport are the same. It's great to see how much this sport has grown," he said.

The experience of going before groups of people to promote something he felt passionate about helped Dr. Borlaug later in life when he had to address the leaders of many different countries. He used those life skills that he learned through wrestling to become one of the most politically savvy plant pathologists. His 20 years of research led to the production of a high-yielding, short-strawed, disease-resistant wheat plant that would grow in Third World countries. He organized teams of scientists from Africa, Asia, and Latin America to return to their own countries to plant the wheat and feed the hungry.

"Battling for economic support was incredibly challenging. I had to go before ministers of agriculture, ministers of finance, presidents, and other world leaders. There were some tough situations and so much depended on how I maneuvered economic policies that needed to be applied. I often thought if I had the courage to go out and wrestle against top wrestlers in the country, then I could go out and get this done," he said. "During the 61 years that I worked and lived in Third World countries, I trained hundreds of scientists. I applied the same spirit I learned from wrestling. You have to always give the best that you have. It takes people of courage to get the job done. That's the toughness."

When Dr. Borlaug worked in Third World countries, he stayed in shape by doing a lot of walking through acres of experimental plots and farms. When he resided in Mexico in 1955, he introduced Little League baseball to the country. He also introduced pony leagues and colt leagues and did a lot of fishing, hunting, and walking.

He still travels the world with hopes of resolving existing agricultural issues. "I'm still in surprisingly good physical condition. I'm one of the only ones left from the early forces that helped food-deficit nations," he said.

He believes wrestling helped set his priorities of staying in shape and working hard as important. "I think, first of all, that wrestling is good for you from the standpoint that you have to maintain your health and physical well-being. In addition, wrestling teaches you to build strong character on your own. When you wrestle, you own the mat. You have to go out there and get it done. That carries over into everything else that you do.

"Wrestling taught me to depend on myself in times of crisis. I found that in my own work and research I was constantly dealing with the unknown. I had to fight through things. Having that drive proved to be valuable in my application of getting new technology and dealing with bureaucrats and people at high levels. Things can get pretty lonely when you're playing for big stakes. It is difficult getting rid of the red tape to get new technology applied. Once you get things going, though, what a difference it makes. India and China are different countries than before the wheat was grown there. When you make a major breakthrough in food-hungry nations, then other things start to happen," he said.

From the 1960s–80s, countries such as India, China, and Pakistan were producing only enough to feed their own people. After some bad harvests and diseases, the food supply diminished. Dr. Borlaug's work helped make a difference in getting the agriculture moving in a positive direction. Now he is concentrating his work efforts in Africa, south of the Sierra.

"They're cursed with a shortage of infrastructure," he explained. "There are no roads and no rivers, so they can't move things. They need to build roads to have schools and set up medical clinics. They need to knock down social barriers and religious barriers. There's social chaos and that's the fate of Africa. This country suffered worse than any other country during the Cold War. I feel strongly that if we want a stable world it won't be built on hunger and misery."

Not only does Dr. Borlaug still work with Third World countries, he also lectures at Texas A&M University. His message to today's college students is a strong one.

"I tell people that the one thing that shocks me is to see how complacent we are in our high standard of living. I don't see students who are overly concerned with their studies. People are okay with mediocrity. I see such a lack of initiative today. People need to find out what drives them. It isn't a question of academic grades. Are you reading across many disciplines? Are you rubbing elbows with people from all walks of life? I tell students that they have to develop their talents, don't waste them. Stretch yourself and reach for the stars. Keep studying, even in later life. You need to get some stardust on your hands while you're making a difference for the well-being of humankind throughout the world," Dr. Borlaug said.

When you wonder just how Dr. Borlaug maintains the pace that he does, he simply answers, "When you look at miserable people in miserable situations, then you have to go out there and try to do something about it. This is the spirit that I got from competitive sports."

15
Learning from Losing

Coach Tom Brands, University of Iowa

On the long road to success in wrestling, there are many blind curves, bumps, and even some detours along the way. You may feel that your wrestlers are working hard and having some success both individually and as a team. That's what it's all about, isn't it? It's inevitable, though, that you will, at some point, be stopped at the tollbooth.

Are you paying the price?

It seems like a simple enough question, on the surface anyway. But when a coach has an elite wrestler vying to place in a tournament, gunning for a championship, or struggling to win a big match, there is only a 50 percent chance he will win.

When he wins, the feeling is great. When he loses, that's when a coach has to take a closer look at the situation.

How should a coach address a major upset? How do you get your athlete to move on after a loss?

Tom Brands, Olympic gold medalist in 1996 and head coach at the University of Iowa, has a few ideas.

"Rebounding from a loss is not at all easy. If I am the coach, then I need to go back and read everything that went into it. Ultimately, what it boils down to: Is the wrestler paying the price? You need to work real hard and you need to work real smart."

By "paying the price," Brands means is the wrestler putting out 100 percent in practice? Is there room to push a little harder?

"The athletes know when they are cutting corners. You have to address it. That's why a coach needs to take the time to know his team. That's the only way that you will know what they are capable of handling.

"If you are not paying the price, then you will not be successful. A wrestler needs to open his eyes and ears to what his coach is saying. As a coach, you can't be totally hard-lined either. A wrestler and a coach need to meet somewhere in the middle. What I am trying to get across here is that a coach needs to be very flexible with his methods of communication. You have your philosophic approach, but leave room for flexibility. That's the 'Gable principle' where you have

University of Iowa coach Tom Brands looks at his athletes as complete people.
(Photo courtesy of Virginia Tech Sports Information Department.)

Tom Brands left Virginia Tech to take over the University of Iowa Hawkeyes in 2006.
(Photo courtesy of Virginia Tech Sports Information Department.)

to read each athlete and implement communication tactics based on what you know about the athlete," Brands added. "Part of paying the price is taking care of your body by getting proper rest, nutrition, and living the right lifestyle."

A wrestler and a coach need to leave room for the idea that there can and will be the occasional freak match where the result is an unexpected loss. Even in the event of a freak match, however, the emphasis should be placed on where the mistakes were made. Reviewing a videotape of the match is a useful way to learn from any loss. A coach can review the videotape to see if he can pinpoint if the wrestler got beat in a certain area and then go over it with the wrestler.

"That's why I was successful. I had an uncanny ability at not making the same mistake twice. I had an uncanny ability to know why and when I got beat and made sure I did not repeat it," Brands said.

"Some of the wrestlers you coach can be hardheaded. You have to go over their mistakes again and again," continued Brands. "Every day you are building your athletes. You do not let a day go by without reminding them of what is important in their development. They need to know they are being held accountable so that they are conscious of what they are doing. There are a lot of coaches who get worn down by the mistakes they see in the practice room. Don't shake your head and just walk away from the situation. I feel very

strongly that if you see a mistake, stop the action and address it immediately. You have to let the wrestler know that these mistakes are never okay. A coach needs to be very detail-oriented. You have to be a perfectionist.

"If you have an athlete who doesn't seem to catch on, do you think he is doing it intentionally? No. It's because he doesn't know any better. That's why you are the coach, so you can show him how it's done."

Brands has studied great leaders in history. He says that great leaders always give credit to others when things go well and take responsibility when things go wrong. "Any good leader does that. It's a universal, timeless, biblical principle," he said.

Brands is in tune with his wrestlers as complete people, not just the wrestling side of an athlete's life. "I want to make sure each wrestler feels good about himself and his future, both during the time they are here and after they leave. They need to feel good about where they are headed in life. When they are involved in my program they know that I am helping to shape them in wrestling and beyond. That's meaningful."

Tips from Tom Brands

1. As soon as the match is over, let the wrestler cool off. Once he cools off, go over and talk to him. Keep your eyes on him, making sure he doesn't sneak away or do something he will regret later. Don't avoid him, that's for sure.
2. Review the videotape of the match and pinpoint where the mistakes were made.
3. Work with the wrestler in practice to avoid making the same mistakes twice.
4. Don't let a single day go by without talking about the essentials. These wrestlers are in your program so they are your responsibility. Don't make excuses.
5. The buck stops with the coach. When the athlete wins, you give him all the credit for getting it done. When he loses, the coach shoulders that responsibility, to a point, without compromising the accountability of the athlete.

16
Running a Tournament

Ken Kraft, Father of the Midlands Tournament

There's a sports question in the board game Trivial Pursuit that asks: "Who was the first person to coach his brother to an NCAA championship?"

The answer: Coach Ken Kraft of Northwestern University. Kraft has been around wrestling for a long time. He became Northwestern's head coach in 1957 at the age of 22. Three years later he coached his brother, Art, to an NCAA championship, a feat that went unmatched for 34 years.

"I was teaching at a local high school when the Northwestern athletic director called me and offered me the coaching

Ken Kraft, former coach at Northwestern University, is the founding father of the prestigious Midlands Tournament.
(Photo courtesy of Northwestern University Sports Information Department.)

position. I remember being told by someone that you don't know when you're going to get the opportunity to coach in college. So I took over the program and worked on getting my master's degree at the same time," Kraft explained.

Meanwhile, Art was drafted into the Korean War, where he went through four months of training. Then he served as a military policeman in Seoul for two years. When he returned to the United States, he went to Northwestern to finish his college degree and to wrestle.

"Art was the guy who made us believe in Northwestern wrestling. He was a clean-living guy who got the job done. We learned through him that Northwestern could compete in the NCAA," Kraft said.

The time the elder Kraft spent coaching his brother was a high point in his life. The brothers had a very close relationship until Art died from cancer at 52. Kraft has struggled with the death of his brother and has had difficulties understanding why this man who was so good was taken away.

"I was struggling with his passing. Someone told me that there are no answers to my questions, but they told me Art was selected to do good things elsewhere. It helps to think those thoughts," Kraft said. "It set the tone, and I worked from there."

Kraft worked diligently to put a wrestling program together that Northwestern could take pride in.

"I felt we could recruit from the Midwest. I knew I could get key people from Illinois. Illinois has good high school wrestling. I went to Oklahoma, Ohio, and Pennsylvania. I tried to identify the people who have the drive to succeed. The No. 1 factor is determination. A wrestler has to have determination, good skills, and natural abilities," he said.

Kraft already had a vested interest in the wrestling program because he had wrestled for the Wildcats where he won a Big 10 title and Northwestern's Medal of Honor. He knew from personal experience what it takes to get through the rigors of athletics and academics.

"I'm impressed with young people who have the will to succeed and can balance it with the life around them. My goal for all of the wrestlers that I coached was that hopefully when they walked out of the wrestling room they would go on to enjoy life. It's important to find the right balance. You can't go halfway," Kraft said.

Not only did Kraft build Northwestern's wrestling program and create the Midlands Tournament, he also served on the board of directors for USA Wrestling from 1965–80. In addition, he presided over the dedication of the National Wrestling Hall of Fame in 1976, and he was the 1976 USA Wrestling Man of the Year. He was also one of the founders of the Wildcat Wrestling Club for youth wrestlers.

"My philosophy is the most important thing that I am going to do is the next thing that I am going to do," he said.

It was that winning attitude that carried him through a 52-year career at Northwestern. Perhaps his greatest accomplishment, however, is that he is the founding father of the Midlands Tournament, a coveted holiday tournament that attracts the most noteworthy wrestlers.

Kraft got the notion to start a Midwestern tournament when he drove his team home through the snow from a tournament at Wilkes College in Pennsylvania. He knew wrestling in the Midwest was strong and that it deserved its own local tournament.

"Driving the long hours home through the snow made me think that we needed to start a tournament in the Midwest. I knew I needed to make it happen," he said. In 1963 the tournament was founded, and it has become the king of open tournaments.

"I'm a believer in spending a lot of time preplanning. I pay a lot of attention to detail. I make sure that we always remember that the tournament is for the competitors. It's all for the wrestlers. I felt that

if we put out a quality product, then the wrestlers would have a positive experience," Kraft said.

A big part of wrestling tournaments, besides the competition itself, is the spectators. Without fans, the tournament would not be as exciting. Kraft said that handing out lots of bracket sheets throughout the tournament keeps the spectators drawn into the event.

"You need fandom. Ultimately, it helps the wrestlers," he said.

The Midlands Tournament started out small with only three mats in a YMCA in Illinois. It was not an instant success, but Kraft worked on getting some of the big name schools at the time to come. The University of Michigan came, Northwestern, and then the Iowa schools followed.

"We had a lot of good luck and good fortune over the years with building this tournament to what it is today. In the early days we started to attract top-level wrestlers. It became a very difficult tournament to win," he said. Kraft continues to serve as one of the tournament directors.

A major part of Kraft's success with the tournament is his band of volunteers. He looked around to pinpoint the best people who could handle the small details, from scorekeepers and referees to concession stands and other maintenance tasks.

"If you're running a tournament, you have to understand your people. Ask yourself, who are the best? Then go out and bring them in. We discovered a group of dedicated people who help to cover the little details that make the big picture complete," he said.

As the Midlands Tournament grew in popularity, so did the size of the crowds. Kraft knows the importance of maintaining order, especially with crowd control, and keeping the environment safe and user-friendly for all participants.

"We must always remember the fans. There's a tendency to walk into the arena at a tournament and all you see is people standing around the mats crowding all of the floor space. You have to maintain order. You have to keep everyone in the stands, and no one should be allowed down by the mats," he advised.

Kraft said that through the years they have tried different things to make it an interesting tournament. One year they incorporated a new rule that the first wrestler to get 12 points wins.

"The fans really loved it, but the coaches did not like it. They were at this tournament to prepare for an NCAA championship. They weren't interested in wrestling with a different set of rules. We listened and took the rule out the following year," Kraft said. "We've experimented a little, but we always listen to what the coaches think. They know what's best for the wrestlers."

Another innovation Kraft implemented was a variety of awards at the tournament. One special award is the Champion of Champions where the entire group of winners vote for their colleague that they think is the best wrestler.

"It's about representing the sport of wrestling. Dan Gable won the outstanding wrestler award back in his day. He helped to make the tournament what it is today," Kraft said.

When Kraft reflects on his time spent building his program at Northwestern and establishing the premier Midlands Tournament, he is proud of his efforts.

"When you're building a program and establishing a tournament, it's a matter of seeking every opportunity. You can't devote your time to something that doesn't give you a big return," he said.

Ken Kraft's Tips on Running a Tournament

1. Understand your volunteers. Bring in the best to help out. A group of dedicated people can help to cover the little details that make the big picture complete.
2. Spend a lot of time preplanning, and pay attention to detail. Remember that the tournament is all for the wrestlers. If you put out a quality product, then the wrestlers will have a positive experience.
3. You need fandom. Ultimately, it helps the wrestlers. Give out bracket sheets as soon as they become available to draw the fans into the competition.
4. Maintain order. Spectators should not be standing around the mats crowding all of the floor space. No one should be allowed down by the mats; keep everyone in the stands.
5. You can experiment a little with the format, but always listen to what the coaches think.

17

A Call to Serve Others

Father John McLaughlin

It was a typical New England February with cold weather, snowy landscapes, and wrestlers heating up to battle for top honors at the state level. For a young high school coach who took a dismal program and turned it into a 17-1 league championship team, the season should have been the *best* of times. Instead, in a matter of seconds, a patch of ice in the road created a nightmare that changed lives forever. In the blink of an eye, the glory season ended.

It became the *worst* of times.

That horrific automobile accident in 1986 claimed the lives of two wrestlers and left another one paralyzed. It sent a young wrestling coach down a path of faith-seeking, inner-strength

reform, and a desire to help others in their times of great need. Woburn High School coach John McLaughlin took this tragic event and the difficult days that followed as a sign that there is so much more to life.

He became a man on a mission.

He left coaching to become Father John McLaughlin, Catholic priest.

When he was a student at Boston College, McLaughlin stayed busy pursuing his studies and competing on the wrestling team. Upon graduation in 1980, his greatest desire was to be a millionaire so he ventured into real estate sales where he was well on his way to business success. His passion for wrestling, though, pulled him in the direction of coaching. He was the assistant wrestling coach at Woburn High School in Massachusetts, his own high school alma mater, and then became the head coach there in 1982. In eight years as head coach, he compiled a 109-32-1 dual meet record and won two league titles. He coached two state champions as well.

When he began as the head coach, the program used an old leftover mat from Harvard University and the warm-up suits were hand-me-downs from the track team. The team collected more than $40,000 for new uniforms, a mat, and improved equipment.

As he split his time between sales and coaching, McLaughlin was thrilled to see the program turn its losing seasons into a winning tradition. The program grew from 16 athletes to 92 wrestlers and McLaughlin was there to coach his younger brothers Gary, Donny, and Keith. Keith became Woburn High's first New England champion.

"When wrestling is in your blood, it's there for life. No matter what you do, you can't get it out of your system," he said.

McLaughlin continued to enjoy success with his teams, mostly because he established a feeder system by bringing ninth graders into the program and because he brought in an assistant coach to help manage the numbers of wrestlers. At the end of the 1986 season, Woburn (17-1) won its first Middlesex League Championship and its first sectional championship and placed fourth in the state. Woburn was off to the New England Championship where some of the wrestlers were bumped out of the tournament early and some moved on to the next round of matches. The wrestlers who were eliminated decided to leave and go to the Medford versus Woburn hockey game. That was the last time the wrestling team would all be together.

On the way home from the hockey game, as McLaughlin shares the story, the car hit a patch of ice and crashed into a tree. There were six people in the car, four of whom were wrestlers. Two wrestlers, Shawn Gillis and Paul Carroll, died instantly. Wrestler John Turner was in a coma with an arm and leg so shattered he would never use them again. Another wrestler, Tim Donovan, broke his C3 and C5 vertebrae and was told he would never walk, talk, or breathe on his own again.

"I got home from the tournament at one in the morning, and I got a call with the news. That was a very difficult time for everyone involved. They were all great kids," McLaughlin said. "I started working with the families and the two boys. I was trying to do anything I could to help them. What I found in return is that it helped my own faith."

McLaughlin made sure that the two boys who lost their lives would never be forgotten. He raised the funds to erect a statue of St. Jude at the local church along with a stone plaque containing their names. He also had their names attached to the first league championship banner that hangs at the school.

Father John McLaughlin coached Tim Donovan at Woburn High School in 1986. A car accident claimed the lives of two Woburn wrestlers and left Donovan paralyzed.
(Photo courtesy of Father John McLaughlin.)

In time, Donovan's father brought his son to the practice room. McLaughlin helped to keep Donovan's spirits up and worked on helping him regain movement in his arms. Eventually, Donovan could breathe on his own again and he could stand up with braces on his legs.

"Timmy had amazing strength. He refused to believe that this was it for him. He prayed every night that God would help him come back," he said.

McLaughlin explained that Donovan was not a great athlete, but he was a very determined wrestler. Prior to the accident, he wrestled in the sectionals and lost a match 15–2 in which he partially separated his shoulder. Since he had already qualified to go to the state tournament, he was advised to rest his shoulder to prepare for that competition.

"He said he wanted to wrestle in his next match [in the sectionals] even though he had already placed, so I talked it over with his dad and we gave him permission. He went out there with his bad shoulder and beat the other kid 3–2. That right there shows you his will to succeed," McLaughlin said.

His will to succeed is what helped Donovan on his long rehabilitation road. As McLaughlin continued to reach out to his former wrestler, the two grew closer in friendship.

"We worked every night in the wrestling room trying to improve his grips and other things. At the same time we were working on his faith, too," he explained. "But what I realized was how much stronger his faith was than mine."

During one of their conversations, Donovan asked his coach if he had heard of the shrine to the Blessed Virgin Mary in Medjugorje, Bosnia-Herzegovina, and if he believed that a person could be miraculously healed by visiting the shrine. There were reports of apparitions of Mary since 1981, and millions of people of all faiths had visited Medjugorje. A worship pavilion had been built on a mountain overlooking the town, which thousands of pilgrims visit each day.

"I told him I didn't really believe in it, but that if he believed, then I would take him there. So that's what I did. There had to be over 200,000 people there visiting this little village. It was at that point that I realized there is so much more to life. At the time, I was into real estate and buying toys and all that. Then it occurred to me that I have another purpose here. I thought I was taking Timmy there, and it ends up that he is the one who helped me," McLaughlin said.

Donovan graduated from Bentley College, earned his certified public accountant (CPA) designation, and now helps out with the youth program in Woburn. He is also the first person in Massachusetts history to get a driver's license with a C3 and C5 disability.

"His story is greater than my story," McLaughlin said.

After that first trip in 1988, the two returned to visit the shrine again in 1989 and 1990. It was those trips that helped McLaughlin accept what had happened and to view life and death differently. McLaughlin left coaching in 1991 and entered St. John's Seminary in Boston where he studied to become a priest. Although his prime directive is the priesthood, Father McLaughlin still keeps his hand in wrestling as he occasionally helps out individuals involved in the sport.

"I was busy being a priest. A coach that I knew brought a struggling wrestler to me to try to help him out. He was a good wrestler, but things didn't seem to be working out for him. He took out his wrestling gear, but before we even worked out I started talking to him. I realized pretty quickly what his problem was. He had zero self-esteem. I thought we would be drilling, but instead we ended up talking for two hours," he explained.

So Father McLaughlin put together a plan for the struggling wrestler: go to church every Sunday and then come work out. He told him that he was a great athlete, but he needed to stick to the plan. The plan worked as the wrestler went on to win the state. He became a New England champion, as well as a prep school and public school All-American.

Father McLaughlin has many athletes to whom he lends a helping hand, and he still helps out with the Foxboro wrestling program.

"I help wrestlers out all the time. I had one kid that I worked with. He was living life the wrong way, and I told him I wouldn't coach him unless he tried to turn his life around. He came to me and told me he would change his life around. He worked hard. He got beat up with wrestling in the beginning, but now he is doing great. He's wrestled for West Virginia," he said.

Father McLaughlin enjoys combining his duties as a priest with his keen interest in sports. He has also been a "prayer specialist" for the New England Patriots at various times.

"I am 9-0 on my blessings for the Patriots. The first time that I was asked to do it, I went to a certain spot to say the pregame prayers and all of a sudden this light went on. I knew it was the right spot to pray so I go to the same spot every time I'm there," he said.

While the coaching side of Father McLaughlin will always be a part of him, he is amazed by the number of wrestlers whose weddings he presides over, whose babies he baptizes, and who continually intersect in his life.

One is John Turner, who survived the car accident, came out of the coma, and is now fully rehabilitated.

"He's a detective now. I did his wedding and baptized his two children," Father McLaughlin said.

"Wrestling changes lives. The sport teaches you how to overcome obstacles. I really think that if you apply what you learn from this sport, then you can overcome anything. When a wrestler goes through all that training and competition, he's being coached to be a champion in life. This sport gives people the inspiration to do things," he said.

18

The Will to Overcome Tragedy

Timothy Donovan

When Timothy Donovan was a senior at Woburn High School, he was the All-American kid enjoying life and having success as a varsity wrestler in Massachusetts. That was until a bad car accident claimed the lives of two of his friends and left him paralyzed. The quick turn of events changed his life forever, and the lessons he learned as a teenager in the wrestling room carried him through the toughest years of his life.

"At the time, I was wrestling in high school and I had the whole world ahead of me. I felt invincible. Never once did I think about how wrestling was going to affect me later in life. When I was in the car accident and I became a quadriplegic,

Timothy Donovan was a hard-working high school wrestler who was paralyzed in a car accident at the end of his senior season.
(Photo courtesy of Timothy Donovan.)

I needed to use all the things that I learned in wrestling to help me cope. Hard work, determination, discipline, and believing in myself all came into play right away," Donovan said.

Wrestling, Donovan shared, is the toughest sport because it forces you to react to situations and you learn instantly whether you made the right decision or the wrong one. He gives credit to the sport for preparing him for the biggest challenge of his life.

"It's like life. Wrestling forces you to learn to survive. You can use what you learn from the sport in your everyday life. I know so many wrestlers who know how to prepare and approach so many different things in life," Donovan said.

From the moment he awoke in the hospital and began to realize that his physical abilities had been severely altered, Donovan said he was supported and encouraged by his family whose unwavering commitment pulled him through his most challenging moments. In addition to his family members, the person who was always there for him was John McLaughlin, his high school wrestling coach.

"He was always right there with me. He spent many, many days with me just sitting and talking and offering words of encouragement. He made sure that I still believed in myself, that I could overcome what happened to me. Twenty years later we're still friends, and I still call him 'Coach.' He has been one of the most influential people in my life," Donovan said.

McLaughlin was there to offer inspiration and encouragement, and he pitched in with physical therapy and rehabilitation, too. Donovan found his coach to be the perfect person to share his ideas with. When he had the notion to travel to visit the shrine at Medjugorje, his coach found a way to make it happen. While they were staying in the small village in the homes of some of the residents, they spent a lot of quiet time in deep reflection.

"That trip impacted all of us, but it impacted Coach the most. We went into the trip with an open mind. We saw people from all over the world. It was a very strong experience to go there and reflect on our own lives and situations. I felt a spiritual healing," explained Donovan. "That was when Coach decided to give up his own life to become a priest so that he could help other people."

Donovan said the same qualities that made Coach McLaughlin a special wrestling coach make him a dynamic priest. He is a regular person who is easy to talk to and will go to great lengths to reach out to people in need.

"He was a tough coach, but he never showed favoritism. He encouraged everyone, and he motivated us to do a lot of extra work on our own. He always said that where there's a will, there's a way. He taught us how to visualize our matches and how to create mental toughness," Donovan said. "Those were the things I needed to overcome my own predicament."

While Donovan was involved in a physical therapy program, he had weekly meetings with his doctors at an outpatient facility. One day, despite the impressive progress that he had made, a doctor told him that his therapy was over because the therapists thought they had done everything they could for him.

"They told me that I needed to move on and live my life by getting involved in my community. I was devastated that the doctor told me there was no more progress to be made. I told this to Coach and he asked me if I believed what the doctor told me. I said absolutely not," Donovan recalled. "Then Coach told me that it was up to me to make things happen and that I had to use what I learned in wrestling to succeed. He told me to make goals and work hard to

achieve them. He told me to use the doctor's words as a piece of motivation."

Donovan spent some time working with doctors at the Miami Project, a research center for patients with spinal cord injuries in Florida. There he engaged in a progressive physical therapy program, which helped him regain some of his physical independence again. He still uses the physical therapy regimen that he learned at the Miami Project.

"I remember being in the hospital, and Coach told me that I have to believe in myself. He was adamant that I had to stay positive and stay motivated. He told me to use what I have to help myself move on. He pointed out to me that although I was surrounded by people who cared about me, there would be times when I would be all alone. It was in those times, he said, that I couldn't allow myself to give up. Coach was right. I went leaps and bounds beyond what the doctors had initially predicted for me," Donovan said.

Donovan eventually went on to earn a degree from Bentley College and to become a certified public accountant in Massachusetts.

Timothy Donovan used the work ethic he developed in wrestling to overcome his disabilities and graduate from Bentley College. Father John McLaughlin (right) was Donovan's high school wrestling coach who encouraged him through some difficult times.
(Photo courtesy of Timothy Donovan.)

"If I had stopped my rehabilitation at the point the doctor told me to move on, I never would have gotten back on my feet to the point where I now can walk extended distances with crutches and for 20 to 30 minutes at a time on a treadmill. This one accomplishment alone has made a major difference in my health and continued confidence in making more physical progress," he said.

Donovan currently works for the City of Woburn as an assistant treasurer collector. He also volunteers in the youth wrestling program in Woburn, where he offers assistance in fundraising and scheduling.

"I enjoy giving back to the sport because I got so much out of it. I like to see other kids grow up with wrestling. It's not like any other sport. After I was in the accident, the support from the wrestling community was amazing. The letters of encouragement helped a lot. It meant so much to me," he said.

It has been two decades since the accident, but for both Donovan and his coach, it seems like it happened yesterday.

"I can't believe it's been 20 years. There's no doubt that being paralyzed is what I know. This has always been extremely difficult for me, but I have been so fortunate because I am surrounded by family and friends who care," Donovan said.

"I have needed a lot of assistance because I lost a lot of my independence. I used what I learned in wrestling to work through this. No matter what your situation is you have to take care of yourself. You have to make time to work out. You have to continue to set goals for yourself. I have done a lot of the things that I had always planned to do, but there are still more things I hope to do. My ultimate goal is to become fully independent again," he said.

And there's no doubt he will get there—he has the heart of a wrestler.

19

The Year-Round Wrestler

Jim Zalesky, Former University of Iowa Coach and Wrestler

The days of the three-sport athlete seem to be waning. There is pressure on young athletes to specialize in a sport early. In America today, society sees no beginning and no end to any of its sports seasons. Gone are the days of hanging up the football cleats to make way for the basketball season. Instead, fall soccer rolls right into winter indoor soccer, which moves back outside for the spring and summer seasons. This overextension of seasons rings true with just about every sport.

Although the trend in sports is to go year-round with one sport, many collegiate coaches would like to see the return of

Above: Jim Zalesky, former coach at the University of Iowa, talks strategy with a Hawkeye wrestler.

Right: Coach Jim Zalesky both wrestled and coached at the University of Iowa.
(Photos courtesy of University of Iowa Sports Information Department.)

the three-sport athlete at the high school, junior high, and youth league levels. Coaches believe that young athletes can benefit from the cross-training that participating in a variety of sports can provide.

There are many wrestlers who have opted to make wrestling their prime athletic directive, which is generally okay, provided there are goals, supervision, and an overall plan. Jim Zalesky, former head wrestling coach of the University of Iowa Hawkeyes, has some insight on this subject.

"I feel that it depends on what level you're at if you decide to train year-round. I think it's healthy to do other sports. I am not a believer in doing just one sport. You can certainly focus on wrestling, but take the time to do other sports and enjoy yourself," Zalesky said.

For a high school wrestler, self-evaluation is key to knowing what moves to make in the off-season. In order to make a jump or break out of a plateau, a wrestler has to decide whether he wants to train more or keep going with competitions.

"You need to keep an eye on the area of your wrestling that needs the most improvements. You have to ask yourself if you need to learn more technique and learn more wrestling or if you need to shift your

focus to more combative wrestling. You might even find that you're lacking in the mental aspects of the sport. It's good to get some advice from a knowledgeable coach," he said.

There are all types of summer camps available in most states. Before you sign up, make sure a camp is being instructed by reputable wrestling coaches. Some camps focus on technique, some are for beginner levels, and some are for the more advanced, competitive-level wrestler. Make sure you do your homework, know what you want, and make a plan. Some camps are strictly for very intense wrestlers and are physically demanding.

"Some of the camps in the off-season are designed to be so tough that it gets you to train to see how hard you can push yourself. Sometimes you build up walls with what you can and can't do. Once those walls are built, a coach has to break them down by pushing you. That's the mental aspect of wrestling," Zalesky said.

For every wrestler, there has to be a time when you allow yourself to take a break from competing, even if you are a year-round wrestler. All too often, a wrestler can compete too much and not be fresh for the big competitions. Each individual is different, so there is no magic formula that applies to everyone to determine when to take a break.

"My philosophy is that there is only so much competition in you. You know what your peaks are during the year, and you train to hit those peaks. During the actual wrestling season, you train to get to your goals. Once the season is over, though, your body needs to rest. You just can't go out and wrestle hard every single day," Zalesky said.

The off-season is a time for learning, lifting, and getting stronger. "I call this the building and learning phase. This is the time to build yourself up and learn the sport," he said.

Many wrestlers focus on weight lifting in the off-season, but Zalesky feels it is a good idea to lift twice a week during the regular season. "A lot of times, when guys are trying to lose weight, they feel tired and skip the lifting. When you're in training you have to get your lifts in. It's an important time. It helps to maintain and increase your strength during the season," he said.

Here again there is no exact answer as to how and when a wrestler should work in his lifts. Zalesky recommends lifting around competitions and going twice during the week, perhaps having one lift heavier and one lift lighter.

"It's easier not to lift because a lot of times you have to do it on your own. I think that if you condition and get your lifts in, this can help in preventing injuries because it helps you to stay strong," he said.

There's no doubt that wrestling is a sport that demands high levels of self-discipline. Those people, like Zalesky, who have been involved in the sport for a long time, have witnessed the character-building that takes place.

"The sport teaches you to make sacrifices so that you can achieve your goals. It's all about the sacrifice. You can't eat and drink what you want whenever you want it. It's a one-on-one battle that leaves you out there all by yourself. When you're done with wrestling you are already ahead of most people because of the intense lessons that you have learned. There is no teammate to pass the ball to. It's up to you to wrestle the whole match," he said.

Jim Zalesky's Favorite Drill

The Penetration Drill

"I like the penetration drill because you can practice it by yourself at any time. The penetration step has to be second nature. You have to be comfortable doing it. If you're not good at it, then go practice it three times a week. Just go up and down the mat. Visualize the step leading to takedowns as you're drilling it. You need to visualize an edge for yourself so that when you go out on the mat you believe it. You need to be thinking things like *I'm good at technique*, or *I'm in better shape*, or *I'm strong on my feet* or whatever you feel it is. There has to be something that puts you one step ahead of everybody else."

20
Building Team Unity

Coach Greg Strobel, Lehigh University; Coach T. J. Kerr, California State University, Bakersfield; and Coach Tom Borrelli, Central Michigan University

Greg Strobel: Get a Hobby

You can always learn something if you have an open mind. When you close your mind, well, then that's when you are not advancing anymore. Lehigh University coach Greg Strobel certainly challenges his wrestlers in the wrestling room with demanding workouts. He also works with them outside of this sport, insisting each of his wrestlers have a hobby that has nothing to do with wrestling.

"That's one of the ways I get to know my wrestlers as individuals. I want to know what their interests are besides school and wrestling. If they don't have a hobby, then I help them to find one. It can't be all about wrestling and schoolwork," he explained.

There is a fine line between working your wrestlers hard and breaking them. Strobel does not believe in "breaking" a wrestler. He compares it to running a horse.

"Horses love to run and race, but you should never break your horse. My father was a foreman on a ranch, and he taught me a lot about horses. That's what he called a wind-broke horse. If a horse breaks, then he'll never run hard again. I believe the same is true of wrestlers. I don't break an athlete, I just push them to the brink," he said.

One type of practice session that pushes Strobel's wrestlers to the brink is called the 30 × 30 practice. It is a practice that lasts 29½ minutes in which the wrestlers have 30 rounds of 30-second goes each followed by a 30-second rest. If you have a top wrestler who needs an extra push, Strobel will match him up with two partners so that he will always go against a rested opponent, forcing him to dig deeper.

Another practice session is a one-hour go. "One hour of live wrestling is tough. No one wants to be the guy who has to stop to rest," he said.

Lehigh University coach Greg Strobel believes that wrestlers need a hobby to broaden their horizons.
(Photo courtesy of Lehigh University Sports Information Department.)

"I don't believe in using calisthenics during practice to get into shape. I only use those types of things as team-building. My reason is that I don't want the wrestlers to be saving themselves for the sprints and calisthenics at the end of practice. I want them going hard. Then after the practice they do sprints together, and the team captains are the ones encouraging the team to get it done.

"I believe in the element of surprise. For example, in the middle of practice recently, I stopped the practice and said that was it—practice was over. The guys looked at me like, 'That's it?' I said, 'Yes, that's it,' and the point is that you should always go hard and not save yourself for anything."

Strobel believes in running a well-planned, efficient practice that never goes past the two-hour mark. "You can get it done with efficiency," he said.

"Wrestling is a unique sport because it is both a team sport and an individual sport. It is more of a team sport though because you can't wrestle by yourself. You need partners and you need opponents. You are only as good as your partner. I like to say that you need a willing accomplice who will push you hard," he said.

"It's as basic as the concept that steel sharpens steel. Wrestlers need to understand the idea that this is a team sport in that we need to help each other become the best that we can be. The military is good at this. They put you through boot camp, and you go through tough times together. That's what pulls them together. It's the tough times that people remember. When the going gets tough, that's when people find out what they're made of," he explained.

When Strobel is looking at a prospective athlete to wrestle for Lehigh, he focuses on some basic things. "I want to meet the athlete and his parents. I want to know if he has a genuine love for wrestling. I want to know what his hobbies include. I look at their statistics and see how they've done in high school. One of the biggest things that I want to try to find out is if the parents have prepared their child for the path that he is going to take or if they have built the path. That's big. The wrestlers who had their parents smooth everything out for them and help them over every bump generally end up being high-maintenance. My goal once I have them is to make human beings out of them. I want them to be self-sufficient.

"In high school the biggest change is physical maturity. In college, the mental change is huge. In college there is no one telling you what

to do. College is the time period when kids set themselves up with habits that they will carry with them. My goal is to help them develop a lifetime of good habits with eating, the friends they choose, and all the choices they make. Choosing good things sets you up for success in the future. I spend a lot of time trying to show them how to develop good habits," he said.

Part of Strobel's message to his team is that each wrestler needs a significant hobby that does not pertain to wrestling or academics. "That concept really throws some of them. It's a pretty cool thing to do. Everyone needs something where they can psychologically relax. You really need to stop thinking about wrestling all the time."

Strobel has actually taught several wrestlers the art of fly-fishing and tying their own flies. He also feels that it is important for everyone on his team to learn how to golf. He wants them to know golf etiquette, to know when and when not to talk, and to know what all parts of the game are called.

"Learning golf is such a productive thing. You have to know the proper protocol. My wrestlers often graduate and find that it is important to know how to golf for business purposes and fund-raising. Some of my wrestlers get really good at it. I tell them that you can't talk business until you're past the first three holes and always let the other people begin the conversation about business. It's the little things like that," he said.

Wrestling and golf have a lot of similarities, says Strobel. "The mental aspect to both sports is huge. In both sports, good thoughts make good shots. What you think about happens. You need a positive attitude. If you're thinking there is no way I can make this shot before you actually take a shot, then you definitely won't make it. If you keep your thoughts positive and you think you can, then you can make it.

"When you drive the ball in golf, you have to pick the spot you're aiming for before you even swing the club. It's the same in wrestling. You have to think about what you want to do if you want to make it happen. When you tee off, you clear your mind and put the ball out there. Wrestling is the same. It just has to happen because there's no time to think about it.

"Even the frustration level is the same in both sports. Just when you think you have it all figured out, you discover that you really don't have it all figured out," he said.

And when you discover you don't have it all figured out, if you keep an open mind, you may just learn something new.

T. J. Kerr: Wrestling with the Wilderness

Cal State Bakersfield coach T. J. Kerr is an outdoor-wilderness guy. He doesn't hesitate to take his wrestlers into the mountains for team-bonding and personal growth experiences. It is through wilderness adventures, says Coach Kerr, that people can really get to know each other as well as gain a new understanding of their personal strengths and weaknesses. Kerr enjoys breaking from the demands of wrestling and city life as he often goes packing into the Golden Trout Wilderness located in the Sequoia and Inyo National Forests.

"I think there is a correlation between being a wrestler and being an outdoorsman. Both sports take a certain discipline with physical and mental toughness. Wrestlers tend to be hard chargers and when certain situations arise in the wilderness, it's interesting to see if they're smart enough to stop or if they're going to charge up the hill. You can get caught in some storms that make it physically challenging," he said.

Coach T. J. Kerr calls instructions to one of his wrestlers in a match.
(Photo courtesy of Cal State Bakersfield Sports Information Department.)

Not only has Kerr been a wrestling coach for three decades, he also teaches self-defense and outdoor education classes at Cal State Bakersfield. Kerr invites his wrestlers to take his spring outdoor course that he feels serves as a special bonding time for the team.

The students take seven one-hour classes from Kerr, during which he instructs them on camping skills, cooking skills, and safety. The culmination of the course is packing up 8,000 feet carrying a loaded backpack. Not only is it physically and emotionally demanding, but everyone burns a lot of calories as well.

"When my wrestlers take my class, they get so much out of it. I give them a more challenging destination than the other students taking the class. They have to plan the whole trip, coordinate who is bringing what, plan the route, and navigate the trails on their own," he explained.

Kerr sends groups of four into the wilderness where each person is responsible for cooking one major meal. Each packer is responsible for his own lunch and snacks. The common gear can be spread out so that everyone shares in carrying the load. The wrestlers learn to appreciate clean water, cooking over a fire, and how to treat food so it doesn't spoil. Instead of relying on the usual mode of electronic entertainment with television and video games, the wrestlers have to talk to and entertain each other.

"It's a hard-core challenge. They have to learn to hang together. In the wilderness, if you separate, then there is the potential for bad things to happen. This is where you learn to rely on your teammates," he said. "I have found that my wrestlers get a great appreciation for nature, and they learn to work together. They develop a new level of tolerance. It's amazing how tough wrestlers are."

Kerr tells his wrestlers to hope for the best but prepare for the worst. Packing in the wilderness is, in many ways, similar to wrestling

Coach T. J. Kerr's Favorite Drill

"My favorite drill is situations. I put the wrestlers in different wrestling positions and they wrestle live from that specific situation for 15–20 seconds. Then I reverse the wrestlers where the other man is in the situation."

experiences throughout the season. The individual challenges are great, but you need your teammates to rely on.

"The river can be roaring out there, so you have to be very careful. You don't want to make mistakes. When you're navigating, you have to make correct decisions. These are the things that people grow from," he said.

Although Kerr suffers from a bad hip and can't push as hard as he used to, he still goes packing regularly and he enjoys fishing in Canada each summer. "When I'm out in the wilderness, I think about wrestling and how I am managing my team. I have to find ways to manage my team on a low budget. I have to work outside the box," he said. "Being in the outdoors releases a lot of stress. It forces you to relax. I've never run into a bad person backpacking. The people I meet hiking are always relaxed because they're not boxed in by the world. I've met some really cool people in the mountains."

Kerr has done a lot of solo packing where he spends five days in the woods alone. Interestingly, he confirmed that there is a lot of truth to the fact that about one hour before it gets dark, your mind starts to play tricks on you.

"Your mind flips out right before it gets dark. When you are out there alone and it gets dark, you don't realize that you are in the same place when it's bright and sunny out. It is important to know this happens and prepare to deal with it," he said.

His outdoor coping mechanisms help Kerr with his coaching. "I think that certain experiences transfer from one area to another area. If I am in a tough place with coaching, I can relate to some of my packing experiences and successes and transfer it back to wrestling," he said.

Coach Tom Borrelli: Togetherness

Although wrestling often seems like an individual sport, a large part of any program's success is building team unity. Coach Tom Borrelli at Central Michigan University puts a lot of emphasis on developing the team as a partnership.

"We do everything as a team. There are not too many individual workouts. I look for athletes who will fit into this philosophy of being team-oriented and family-oriented," he said.

Central Michigan University coach Tom Borrelli creates a family atmosphere within his program.
(Photo courtesy of Central Michigan University Sports Information Department.)

To help build the family concept, Borrelli likes to include the parents of his wrestlers in his program. Throughout the season, he assigns parents to help out at various tournaments, especially with the food and hospitality.

"We have a group of parents that stay together in a certain area who prepare and bring the food. The purpose is so that our wrestlers have a place to go to be with familiar people and eat good food instead of picking up something at the concession stand. It's very important because it means so much to the wrestlers," he said.

Borrelli also likes to host an open practice where parents can watch and bring food to simulate a tailgate party.

Another factor in developing the team is talking before and after every practice session, which helps keep wrestlers on track and motivated.

"Before each practice I discuss the goals that the team should strive to accomplish during that practice session. Then after the practice I like to do something inspirational. This varies throughout the season. I might talk about something that relates directly to them. I might talk about the power of believing in yourself," he explained. "I

try to inspire the team with something current that relates to what we're doing."

Central Michigan has a nice locker room that Borrelli uses for everything from weigh-ins to team meals. It is the gathering point before and after practices and matches.

"It's very motivating to have teammates pulling for you. Peer pressure can be positive and influential when you know that your teammates care. Wrestlers will work harder because they don't want to let their teammates down," he said. "I feel that the more they like each other and share their goals, they will stand by each other no matter what."

Borrelli also enjoys celebrating the holidays with his wrestlers, including sharing Thanksgiving dinner at his house and having parties at Christmastime.

In the off-season, there are volunteer training sessions led by the team leaders. All of the wrestlers stay at school for the summer. This is a time when the teammates relax and enjoy floating down the river once a week and playing basketball together. Being a part of a competitive program can be fun.

"We are on the bus a lot and we have some fun just doing silly things or playing cards. We try to keep things light and just enjoy each other's company," Borrelli said.

Coach Tom Borrelli's Favorite Drill

Easy-In, Hard-Out

"My favorite drill is called the easy-in, hard-out. We start our wrestlers on their feet doing some hand-fighting. One wrestler is all defense, and the other wrestler is all offense. On the whistle, the offensive guy takes a shot and once he locks his hands around the defensive wrestler's legs, it turns into full-speed wrestling. The drill creates some great scrambles and scoring situations. We have numerous variations to this drill, but the basic concept is to create scoring opportunities repeatedly."

21
Making the Right Call

Dr. Vincent Zuaro, Referee

Dr. Vincent Zuaro has spent his lifetime making the calls. As an official in five Olympic Games, 34 World Championships, six Pan American Championships, and national tournaments spanning 30 years, Zuaro has traveled all over the world as a model of integrity and fair play.

He was the nation's foremost clinician on freestyle and Greco-Roman rules and officiating techniques and has trained more than five thousand referee-judges across the nation and throughout U.S. armed forces in Europe.

"Wrestling is such a blue-collar sport. It's hand-to-hand combat. Whether you're coaching or officiating, there are certain relationships that are built between human beings. From

Dr. Vincent Zuaro officiated 5 Olympic Games, 34 World Championships, 6 Pam Am Championships, and 30 years of national tournaments.
(Photo courtesy of Bruce Curtis.)

those relationships there are so many lessons learned that you take so much away with you," Zuaro said.

Interestingly, so much of Zuaro's life has been spent on the wrestling mat, yet he has never wrestled a single match in his life. He grew up in New York City where there was no opportunity to wrestle, and then he went to Holy Cross on an academic and football scholarship. He played in the 1946 Orange Bowl as an offensive lineman and center on defense where the Crusaders lost to Miami 13–6 in the last 30 seconds of the game.

Zuaro first became involved in wresting as a football coach at Freeport High School on Long Island in 1953. To help his football players stay in shape during the off-season, he decided to start a wrestling team. He attended the Lehigh University summer clinics and took lots of notes to learn about a sport he originally knew nothing about. As Zuaro began to take wrestlers to tournaments, there never seemed to be enough officials. He often stepped in to help, which resulted in a lifetime of officiating and a passion for wrestling. Zuaro founded the U.S. Wrestling Officials Association in 1970 and authored the USA wrestling rule book for 20 years. He was also a school superintendent on Long Island.

Zuaro received the FILA (Fédération Internationnal de Lutte Amateur) cross/star five times, the highest award of international wrestling. He also received the gold whistle for his Olympic and World officiating. In 1984 he was inducted into the Wrestling Hall of Fame, where the referees' room is named in his honor. Four years later, he retired after the 1988 Olympic Games in Seoul, Korea.

"There's a lot of water under the bridge," he said, smiling as he talked about the glory days. As a reminder of his accomplishments, he proudly wears his Hall of Fame ring.

Even at age 81, Zuaro's passion for the sport has not diminished. He never misses a Hofstra University home wrestling match because he lives close to the university, he traveled to Hungary for the 2005 World Championship, and he is in attendance at the NCAA championships every year. Zuaro is a walking encyclopedia of wrestling information, and he appears to be capable of recalling every person he ever met through wrestling.

"I think that the NCAA is stable in its rules and regulations, which are good for the sport. It enables the coaches to coach according to the rules. The NCAA is moving in the right direction," he said. "Internationally, however, the rules change so much that you can't get acclimated fast enough. They're trying to make the sport more attractive to watch, but that's not happening."

Zuaro is credited with putting the international rules into the limelight when he started bringing the information back to the United States from the international competitions he officiated from 1962–70.

"We started to do well internationally once we started to focus on the rules. I think the U.S. needs to revert back to paying attention to the rules again," Zuaro explained. "We can't be arrogant by saying we'll wrestle U.S. style, come what may, because if you're going to play their game then you better learn their rules."

Zuaro does not agree with the current international shortening of the periods to two minutes. "It doesn't work. It diminishes a wrestler's need for skill because there's not enough time to utilize skills. I think the periods should be three minutes each," he said.

For current referees, Zuaro offers some sound advice. "It's not a tough job if you have talent, knowledge of the rules, and you can withstand attacks from coaches," he said. "A referee has to have complete integrity. A referee should never try to console a coach on a call

he made. However, if a ref does realize he made an error, he should recognize it, be the better person, and change the call. That's what gets respect."

With high school and college matches, a referee has a pre-match discussion with the teams before competition. "A ref needs to be sure he makes it clear how he interprets the rules and how they will be enforced in the match. This has to be done so that there is no doubt when the calls are made. The coach should be present during this discussion, too," he said.

Zuaro also has one significant piece of advice for coaches. "A coach should never yell at the official. It doesn't help any situation. The coach should direct his comments to the wrestler with the idea that the message is being heard by the ref. Remember that most refs are either coaches or they were once coaches, so they're not easily influenced by what is being said from the coaches' corners," he said.

Then, as Zuaro strummed the table with the same fingers that signaled points for so many years in so many matches, he laughed and said, "No matter what you do, there are some coaches who blame the refs for everything."

22

The Edge of Mental Toughness

Coach Steve Fraser, U.S. Olympic Greco-Roman Wrestling

Mental toughness is a *learned* behavior, and there are many things a wrestler can do to achieve a high level of mental toughness.

When Greco-Roman gold medalist Steve Fraser addressed a group of Hofstra University wrestling fans, he posed a tough question: "What is mental toughness?"

Members of the audience offered answers. Some suggested mental toughness means being focused and prepared for a match. Some wondered if it means being callous or even ill-spirited at times.

Fraser, who is the U.S. Olympic Greco-Roman coach, said he defines *mental toughness* as being able to get into your ideal competitive state in a snap. It is a state that allows you to feel the most energized, confident, and strong.

"We all experience being nervous before a match. Is being nervous helping you get in your ideal competitive state? No. It's when you have a positive fighting attitude and you're enjoying the struggle," he said.

Some factors that work against mental toughness are fear, a lack of self-confidence, being unprepared, confusion, and fatigue. These are the negative attributes that wrestlers must learn to control to ensure positive energy.

"Wrestlers need to learn to create positive emotions so that they can step out on the mat and say let's go, regardless of what is happening in their lives," he said.

The greatest moment in Fraser's wrestling career came in the quarterfinal round of the 1984 Olympics when he faced Sweden's Frank Andersson, who was favored to win. Andersson had claimed the World Championship in 1979, 1981, and 1982, and he was expected to take the gold medal in the 1984 Olympics.

Steve Fraser developed his own approach to mental toughness during his training for Olympic gold.
(Photo courtesy of Steve Fraser.)

Steve Fraser took the gold medal in the 1984 Olympics.
(Photo courtesy of Steve Fraser.)

"I went to bed the night before the match and I was nervous. I started to focus on all the things that I could control. I didn't think about winning or losing. I knew I could control the tempo of the match. I knew I could go fast. I wanted to make it an exciting match for the home crowd. I visualized my match. I knew I had to defend his straight lift that he was throwing everybody with. I pictured the whole match in my head, and it worked. It took many years to prepare for that match. It was the biggest match of my life," Fraser said.

His advice is that each wrestler needs to identify his own ideal competitive state. That does not mean a wrestler has to go out and win every match. "It means that you are not going to leave any bullets in your gun on that day. You have to give it everything you have," he said.

Fraser has a few practical suggestions that can help a wrestler learn to achieve his ideal competitive state. The first is to keep a wrestling journal, in which a wrestler should record the number of hours of sleep he gets per night. Right before he goes to sleep at night, he should record the time and also record what he ate that day. The wrestler should also write down what his training activity was for that day. Finally, he should make a note about how he felt throughout the day.

"After you keep a notebook for a while, you start to figure out what makes you tick," Fraser said. "You need to track things so that you can look back in your journal and review the weeks when you felt like an iron man. You can see what you were doing and try to get it to happen again."

There are times when you will come to practice and feel lethargic or distracted by the events of the day. You have to learn to catch yourself before you waste an entire practice session by slacking off. Comparisons can be drawn to acting. When the camera begins to film a scene, the actor has to act no matter what is happening in his life. Wrestlers need to learn to be actors as well.

"You have to force your body to look alive. Bring your shoulders back, keep your head up, and put a little skip in your step. Once your body perks up, then your mind will follow," Fraser said.

At the Olympic Training Center, the wrestlers strive to maintain a perfect practice attitude or a no-complaining attitude. This means that no matter what the coach asks you to do, you find a way to get it done.

"You have to prepare your mind to think that no matter what the coach throws at you, it can't break you. You need to think things like *bring it on* and *the more the merrier*. You can't get hung up on somebody cheating or a bad call or somebody not working hard. When you wrestle, nothing the other guy is doing can bother you," he said.

There are times in a practice session when two wrestlers will be battling and one competitor may lose his temper and punch the other wrestler. Obviously, this is against the rules. A normal reaction would be to punch back, but that would be a sign of weakness.

"You have to stay focused and keep wrestling. If you were to punch your opponent back, then it would show that he broke you. When you act like it doesn't bother you, your opponent will know that you are tough. He will know that nothing can break you," he explained.

A coach should put his wrestlers in various adverse situations so that the athletes can practice how to stay focused. For instance, a coach should intentionally make some bad calls during a practice match and then watch how the wrestlers react and offer advice about remaining focused.

A one-hour grind match is another way to develop mental toughness. A grind match is no out-of-bounds, nonstop wrestling that helps to develop "in-your-face" tactics and improve your rhythm. It forces a wrestler to learn to relax and not waste precious energy by being tense. It calls on a combination of staying relaxed and timing when to explode.

"A grind match gets you to be able to pull your moves when the moment of truth comes and you find yourself in a tough situation," Fraser said. "This is where you learn to break your opponent's will to fight. Once you break your opponent, then it becomes like taking candy from a baby."

A wrestler should be open to all possibilities, especially if you need to change your strategy in a match. If you get behind in a match, think to yourself that the score is 0–0 and you keep on fighting.

"Don't give up. You can wear your opponent down if you just keep fighting. You can frustrate your opponent," he said.

Fraser makes it clear that toughness is not something a person is born with. "You have to work at your mental toughness just like you work on your technique," Fraser said. "Don't ever think that you can't achieve your wildest dreams in wrestling."

23

Seize the Moment

Sam Kline, All-American at West Virginia University

Some people might be inclined to say that he is the *luckiest unlucky* man alive. Sam Kline was right where he wanted to be—an Olympic wrestling hopeful with room to improve and the will to work to get to the level he always dreamed about. Kline was in the U.S. residence program at the Olympic Training Center in Colorado Springs working daily on his conditioning and freestyle technique. He was busy training to fulfill his chief ambition.

"I always knew I wanted to go for Olympic gold. I knew I had some distance to go in my freestyle career," Kline recalled.

An NCAA All-American, Kline ended his collegiate career at West Virginia University with a third-place finish at 174 pounds in the 1999 NCAA Championship. He then served as

Sam Kline earned All-American honors when he wrestled for West Virginia University. His Olympic dreams were shattered by a rare illness that almost took his life.

Photo courtesy of West Virginia University Sports Information Department.)

an assistant coach at West Virginia before heading to Colorado to pursue his dream. Internationally, he had success when he won the Henri Deglane Challenge in France in 2000.

Life seemed great until a nagging muscle strain in the back part of his rib started troubling Kline. As any top-level wrestler would do, Kline tried to work through the discomfort so he could quickly return to the mat and resume his weight-lifting regimen. But the pain continued to the point where he eventually went to the emergency room.

Doctors initially thought Kline had strained his back. He had no medical insurance at the time, so he opted not to have an MRI. Kline left the emergency room only to find his life became unbearable. He found that the only thing he could do was sit in a chair for 12 hours at a time and not move. In agony, he finally took some pain medication to ease the discomfort. That allowed him to get to his bed to take a nap, but when he awoke he was completely disoriented. He had no idea how long he had been asleep, and he had a strange, warm tingling sensation from his waist down. When he tried to get out of bed, he realized he had no feeling in his legs.

"I somehow was able to call a trainer at the athletic center, and she came over to help me. She tried to get me into a chair, but she couldn't. I couldn't imagine what was happening to me. I was then brought over to the emergency room where they gave me two MRIs. They showed that I had a massive infection in my spine," Kline recalled.

Incidentally, all of this was happening on Kline's 25th birthday.

The doctors and nurses moved swiftly in preparing Kline for emergency surgery. He felt the whir of energy and heard the serious tone of the doctors' pre-op discussions.

Kline asked the doctor, "Will I be able to wrestle again?"

With a grim expression on his face, the doctor leveled with him, replying, "I don't know if you're going to live."

Sam Kline calls out instructions from the bench as an assistant coach at West Virginia University.

Photo courtesy of West Virginia University Sports Information Department.)

The nurse called Kline's parents to let them know he was undergoing surgery and the prognosis was not good. She mentioned that if he survived the surgery, he could end up a quadriplegic.

The doctors operated immediately, opening him up to let the infection literally ooze out of him. They were stunned to find how enormous the infection was and how quickly it had moved up his spine, through his shoulders, and down his arms. They performed a double-level laminectomy, in which they irrigated the area and cut the spinous process out from his spine.

Doctors estimated that Kline was within *20 minutes* of the infection spreading into his brain and possibly killing him.

The cause of the infection was difficult to identify. It may have been caused by a root canal procedure, or maybe a rib injury triggered internal bleeding that dripped into the bottom of his spine. No one knows for sure. When Kline awoke from the surgery, he was relieved to be alive, but he was informed there was a long recovery ahead.

"When I was told that I couldn't wrestle anymore, I was heartbroken. The doctor explained that my spinal column was weakened and compromised and that I would be at great risk for paralysis if I wrestled. I knew I didn't want to be in a wheelchair for the rest of my life, so I started focusing on my rehabilitation," Kline said.

He defied his doctors' early predictions as he forced himself to sit up in bed and the next day, much to everyone's surprise, started walking down the hallway. Kline took only six months to recover and continued to make improvements for three years after the surgery. There was a lot of guesswork involved in the postsurgery prognosis because each case is individual, but everyone agreed that Kline's age, determination, and great overall physical condition helped in his full recovery.

"I used that time to examine my life a lot. My whole perspective was changed. I realized that we're not guaranteed another second in anything. So often you hear people say, 'I'll do it tomorrow' or 'I'll get to that next year.' I learned that you can't do that. You have to seize the moment and make things count," he said.

While he was in the hospital, there were lots of phone calls and people trying to support Kline. He said the support from the tight-knit wrestling community was incredible.

"It was a wild experience. My phone kept ringing in the hospital. It helped me to recover. I feel that everyone reached out to me, which was so important," he said.

Using the mental toughness that he developed during his wrestling years, Kline focused on his rehabilitation. When he was told he wouldn't walk again, Kline rejected the idea.

"In wrestling you tell yourself that you are going to win under any circumstance. You don't allow negativity into your mind. When people said I wouldn't walk again, what I heard was that I had to work hard so that I could walk again. I was looking for a win out of this scene," he said.

He got more than a victory.

He pushed himself in rehab the same way he pushed himself when he was training for wrestling. Wrestling taught him how to endure painful workouts. Once he was discharged from the hospital, he returned to the Olympic Training Center where he continued his rehabilitation. A new trainer, Laura, had just been assigned to the wrestling team at the center. She worked with Kline through his entire rehabilitation, and a strong friendship developed between them, which eventually led to marriage.

"She was cute, and I definitely would have noticed her without having to almost die," he said laughing. "We got to be friends and got to know each other. I appreciated that. Now we have a daughter, Camryn, and we couldn't be happier," he said.

Laura is studying to become a doctor, and Kline is involved in construction and real estate development in the West Virginia area.

"In many ways, I was lucky. When you have something that slugs you emotionally, it takes time to get over it, but it forced me to get a new perspective on life," he explained. "When I look back on it, I wasn't very far from having my life drastically altered. I was carried into that hospital and left on my own accord. I think I was as lucky as you could get in that situation. The scar on my back wins all the scar contests."

Kline has spent some time traveling to various wrestling camps and clinics speaking to groups about his experience. He shares his story and tries to impress upon wrestlers that the hard work is worth the enormous effort.

"I try to give a message to other wrestlers that they should embrace the difficult aspects of the sport and embrace the tight community. It is fun to be a part of that. I tell them to stick with wrestling no matter how difficult it seems at times because it develops a person at the core," he said.

One thing that wrestling and Kline's life-altering experience taught him was how to look on the bright side of things.

"I did get to wrestle a lot of years and I find that satisfying. I had a hard time with the fact that I couldn't finish my career on my own terms, but that difficulty got less and less hard to deal with. Wrestling taught me to set goals and work hard, which is exactly what I needed to get through this whole experience," he said.

24

The Role of Supportive Parents

Advice from Fathers in the Coaching Corner

Behind many successful wrestlers are parents who have been very supportive through it all. The journey in wrestling can be difficult and, in many cases, an athlete's involvement with the sport affects the whole family. The grueling workout regimen and difficult competitions can take their toll on a wrestler's household because of the demands on everyone's time. Any parent who has endured tournaments knows that the hours of sitting on rock-hard bleachers and battling that foggy "gym-head" sensation is not always easy. The season can be an emotional roller-coaster ride with exciting wins, injury setbacks, wrestle-off losses, and other tough

situations. All of this seems compounded by the critical focus that needs to be placed on nutrition and making weight. Wrestling is a family affair that works best when parents consciously keep the atmosphere positive even in the most difficult moments.

Many wrestling families find a way to make it work, offering support and encouragement to keep their wrestlers on track. One clan that has enjoyed generations of wrestling is the Churella family of Michigan. Mark Churella Sr. was a three-time national champion for the University of Michigan (1974–79) and he was a four-time All-American. He became a distinguished member of the Wrestling Hall of Fame in 1999. He has three sons: Mark Jr., who wrestled for Michigan and graduated in 2002, and Josh and Ryan, who competed on the school's highly ranked 2006 team.

"I was never really sure that any of my sons would wrestle. I was committed to having them involved in athletics, but at the same time they were exposed to wrestling," the elder Churella said.

He explained that his sons were first exposed to the sport when he was the head coach at the University of Las Vegas. There he founded the Las Vegas Invitational, a prestigious collegiate tourna-

Mark Churella, working his opponent's arm, was a three-time national champion for the University of Michigan, 1974–79. The four-time All-American was inducted into the Wrestling Hall of Fame in 1999.
(Photo courtesy of University of Michigan Sports Information Department.)

Ryan Churella works his moves in an early season match during his senior year at the University of Michigan. His parents and grandparents attended all of his matches.
(Photo courtesy of Bruce Curtis.)

ment held in early December. His sons decided on their own to get into wrestling when they were in junior high school.

"Our dynamic is a little different than most families. When they reached the high school level, I became part of the coaching staff so that I could help out. You hear a lot of father-son stories where the child does not want to take the father's advice. I'm happy to say that it has been a positive experience for all of us," said Churella.

His oldest son, Mark, has fond memories of having his dad by his side in wrestling. Their bond is so strong that he even joined his father's business after he graduated so that they could work together.

"My dad had all the accolades in wrestling, but he never pushed the sport on us. He told us he was there to support us 100 percent, and he helped us with proper training, developing mental toughness, and basic fundamentals," Mark said of his father. "I am like a sponge when I'm around my dad. I've always listened to him whether it was with wrestling or now in business. He's a great mentor, father, and coach."

The whole family, including grandparents, have attended many Michigan matches across the country. While the Churellas have a passion for Michigan wrestling, it was never easy watching a family member wrestle.

"That's the only trouble I have, watching my sons. On the conscious level, it's only a match and I have no impact on what they're doing on the mat while it is happening. I get that lump in my stomach and can't get rid of that feeling, and it exacerbates and gets worse until it's over," he explained during the 2006 season. "My wife is also troubled when they wrestle. Emotionally and mentally it kills her. She almost gets ill before their matches. It seems silly, but in that moment, the most important thing is what they're doing."

Churella enjoys the overall process, and he always finds something to review with his boys when the match is over.

"I keep my observations very positive. I am pleased to have had the opportunity to coach all three boys. I'm very blessed. The three of them are very close brothers. I'm a big supporter of the University of Michigan because I grew up 30 miles away and I went there and had so much success. The boys had to make their own choice, but I'm glad they went there," he said.

Churella also noted that wrestling is a great sport for a father to get his children involved in, as long as it is done in a positive, nurturing way. He feels that it is a sport that provides building blocks and self-confidence for later in life. But he also knows all too well the energy and toil it takes to persevere in this sport.

Mark Churella has his arm raised in victory in 1979 where he signals to the crowd that Michigan is No. 1.
(Photo courtesy of University of Michigan Sports Information Department.)

"College athletes go through a difficult journey. A lot of wrestlers dream of being an NCAA champion, but the reality is that it's exceedingly harder and harder. All of the wrestlers are invested in their commitment to succeed. In wrestling and in life not everything is in your hands," he said.

Olympic wrestlers Terry and Tom Brands praise their parents for their constant support while they pursued their wrestling endeavors.

"My dad has an unbelievable mentality. He tells you like it is," Terry said, "and that's how it is in wrestling. If you want something, then you have to go get it. The hardest part is actually doing it. That's where parental support is important."

Both Brands brothers agree that the desire to compete and succeed must come from within each wrestler. "Parents should not push what they want their kids to do. When it comes to drilling and working out, the athlete has to do it, not the parents saying, 'Okay, now it's time to run' or 'Hit the weight room.' I have seen kids being pushed by parents and they succeeded in high school, but once they

Tom Brands watches from the coaches' corner during a Virginia Tech match in the 2005 season.
(Photo courtesy of Virginia Tech Sports Information Department.)

went away to college the self-discipline wasn't there because they never developed it on their own," Terry added.

Terry notes that there is a delicate balance between how involved parents should get in the child's wrestling and when they should step back. "Support is very important. The biggest thing is that if your child gets beaten, you can't yell at him or get down on him. He feels bad enough as it is. You have to remember that he is doing the best that he can."

Jesse Jantzen was a standout wrestler for Harvard whose father, Donald Jantzen, coached him through his high school career at Shoreham Wading River on Long Island. Jantzen captured the first national championship for Harvard in over half a century with a decisive 9–3 win over Zach Esposito of powerhouse Oklahoma State in front of a national television audience and 15,081 fans in St. Louis, Missouri, in March 2004. There were a lot of family members, friends, and fans there cheering for Jantzen. John Harkness, Harvard's only other national champion, in 1938, was also there to watch history being made. The Jantzen family and Harvard fans were not only treated to an NCAA championship, but Jantzen was also awarded the NCAA Outstanding Wrestler Award in 2004.

"Winning that championship was the cherry on top of the sundae," said Jantzen, the proud father, "but the journey was what it was all about for us. I can recall driving to so many different tournaments talking about what is important in life. I think your best bet is giving your kids the gift of time whether they're pursuing sports or music or art or some other endeavor."

Jantzen tailored his career so that he could be more involved in coaching. "If it's important, then you have to make sacrifices," he said.

Jesse, who is training to make the 2008 Olympic team, was the first four-time state champion in New York history. He was a three-time high school All-American and a two-time high school national champ, and he claimed the 2000 National Most Outstanding Wrestler Award. He was also the University World Champion in 2005.

"I used to ask him when he was younger and we were traveling all around, 'Do you think this is too much? Do you think you're missing out on what your friends are doing?' He always told me no, that it was what he wanted to be doing. I think his early successes are what gave him his main drive," the elder Jantzen said.

The Role of Supportive Parents

Jesse fell short in his sophomore and junior seasons as he took third place in the NCAA tournament losing out to top-level wrestlers. "Fortunately, things came through for him. He had knocked on the door twice before, and people really thought he could do it in his senior year. There are an awful lot of talented people at that level. If he had fallen short again, it would have left a lot of questions in his mind," Jantzen said of his son.

Jantzen managed to coach his son and be his No. 1 fan through the years. "I think that if parents are interested in helping their kids enjoy sports, you need to go through it with them and remain positive. I see so many parents who go up to a kid after he loses and tell him 65 things that he did wrong. You have to remember that there will always be a thousand people to knock you down. As parents, your job is helping your child believe in himself. That can be achieved through positive reinforcement," he said.

Jesse relishes his memories of having his dad in the coaches' corner. "I loved it. People might think that it was a situation where the parent is smothering the child, but that wasn't the case with us. He was never the type of coach who did things in a negative way, and he didn't come down hard on me if I didn't do things properly. He also didn't give me special treatment over the other wrestlers, either," he said.

Another wrestling parent, Al Bevilacqua, who was mentioned in a "Seinfeld" episode for being Jerry Seinfeld's physical education teacher at Massapequa High School on Long Island, was also the wrestling coach at the school. His son, Chris, was a two-time NCAA All-American at Penn State where he graduated in 1986.

"I learned from being a coach that the majority of fathers should sit in the highest seat in the gym. All the father wants the child to do is win, right? So that's a distraction to the wrestler. After 50 years of experience, I say that parents are there to encourage, not discourage. Our job is to teach them how to be successful," Bevilacqua said. "Quitting is too easy. Part of the learning experience is to make a commitment and then finish the race."

Bevilacqua implemented a mother's club when he coached at the high school level. He felt that by instructing the mothers about the sport, they could then be more understanding and supportive of their sons' overall wrestling experiences.

"I told parents that wrestling is a great sport for children. They're all winners just by having the courage to go out on the mat to compete in front of people," Bevilacqua said.

Tom Borrelli, the head coach at Central Michigan, coached Jason, his son, through his college career for the Chippewas.

When a coach's son is on the team, it naturally creates a unique situation. Everyone needs to be treated equally on a team, but that can get tricky when one of the wrestlers is your own child.

"I've learned a lot from coaching my son and I have enjoyed it, but I do have to say that it is not easy," Borrelli said.

Naturally, there is a lot that goes on behind the scenes that affect a person socially on a team. There is a fine line between being a supportive parent and being an encouraging coach.

"I'm concerned with his relationships with his teammates. I'm concerned with the team's perception of how I handle my son whether it's positive or negative. I wonder if the guys think I'm too easy or too hard on him. I try to treat everyone on the team as if they were all my sons," Borrelli said.

Coach Tom Borrelli of Central Michigan calls out instructions to his son Jason during one of his matches for the Chippewas.

(Photo courtesy of Central Michigan Sports Information Department.)

Drexel University coach Jack Childs offers advice to one of his wrestlers. After 30 years of coaching and claiming more than 300 victories, Childs treats each wrestler as if he were his own son.

(Photo courtesy of Drexel University Sports Information Department.)

Coach Tom Borrelli's Advice to Parents Who Coach Their Kids

1. Let them have fun when they are young.
2. Success has to come from the child, not from the parents forcing the issue.
3. Don't fight your child's battles because it sets your child up for failure later.
4. Let your child stand on his own two feet and make things happen for himself.
5. Enjoy the time you are spending together.

"I found it difficult when he hurt his knee in the national duals. I had to keep on coaching while he was back with the trainers dealing with the injury. You feel torn because as a parent you want to be there for him, but as a coach I still had other wrestlers to focus on," he explained. "All I know is that I wouldn't miss the opportunity to coach him. It's pretty special."

Drexel University coach Jack Childs has coached the Drexel University Dragons since 1976. He has been a father figure to many student-athletes through the years, and he coached his two sons in wrestling when they attended Drexel.

"Coaching wrestling at Drexel for the past 30 years has been more than a job; it's really been my life. This has been a life-long labor of love. Drexel is a great product as a university, and it is right in Philadelphia, which is a great city. This was a great fit for me, and now I am entrenched here," he said.

He recorded his 300th career victory during the 2002 season. During his coaching tenure, he has had 20 seasons with at least 10 wins. In 2003, Childs was inducted into the Southeastern Pennsylvania Wrestling Hall of Fame. Along with coaching, Childs is also an assistant professor of physical education at Drexel.

"I never felt that I did anything special as a coach, but I make sure I have a great rapport with my athletes. Not only do I recruit the student-athlete, but I also recruit the parents as well. Wrestling is a real family affair here at Drexel. When we travel to a match we get a

50-seat bus. There are a lot of extra seats so we extend the offer to have the parents travel with us, too. I feel that these parents are entrusting me with their sons, and I am like a surrogate father to them for four years. I make sure I focus on life skills, because that is what they will take with them," he said.

Childs makes his expectations clear to his wrestlers right from the beginning.

"I am very old school. I teach them to shake hands and look people in the eye. If a woman comes into the room, you stand up out of respect and offer her your seat if there are no other seats available. When you take a class for the first time, shake your professor's hand and introduce yourself. These are the types of life skills that are so important, and all too often they get overlooked these days," Childs said.

Over the years, Childs has learned that it is important to stress personal management skills to his wrestlers. He believes it sets them up for success in the future.

"One of the biggest things that I ask from my wrestlers is time management. I tell them that if you are early for a practice, then you are on time. If you are on time for a practice, then you are late. If you are late for a practice, then you are locked out of the wrestling room. Instead of wrestling with the team, the late athlete finds himself running in the hallway with 25-pound weights. That usually gets the message across," he said.

Just as a parent would do in a well-run household, Childs establishes rules and expects the athletes to adhere to them. He sets up rules not to make anyone's life unbearable but to teach life lessons.

"I ask my athletes to be respectful of themselves, the coaching staff, other athletes, and other students. I stress that academics come first, tobacco and alcohol are forbidden, and weight management is very important. The piece about weight management is crucial, and I take the approach that this is another lesson for life. Watching your weight forces you to know your body, what you can eat and how much weight training and cardiovascular exercise you require to stay in shape. I am not a control freak, but the team knows the rules and the standards we set. The biggest thing is that no one wrestler is bigger than the team. Some lessons are hard. Whether you win or lose, you don't disrespect yourself and you don't disrespect your opponent," he said.

Jack Childs's Tips for Coaching Your Own Kids

Having coached two sons who wrestled for him at Drexel University, here are some of Childs's tips:

1. Treat all of the athletes the same, even if one happens to be your kid. Try not to be harder or easier on your own child.
2. In the wrestling room, the coach's word rules. There is no time for discussion. When we need to communicate, that takes place after practice and it is done privately. My sons knew that was the deal for them, too.
3. Make sure wrestling is a sport your child wants to do. Don't live your life through your children. This is too tough of a sport to be forced into doing. I think it is the most demanding sport out there. The child has to be committed to it.
4. Your job is to just help all wrestlers live a respectful life.
5. Use the opportunity of coaching your child as another avenue for you to get close to your child. Coaching gives you the opportunity to see what motivates and makes your child tick.
6. Watch carefully how your child interacts with peers. The social factor is a big life skill and that's where you can possibly pick up on things in the wrestling room. How does your child get along with others? Does your child respect others? Is your child liked by their peers? If your child struggles socially, then you can give some extra support and guidance about issues that you might not be otherwise privy to.
7. The parent needs to be professional about what he is doing. Here is where the child has the opportunity to really look up to Dad. The child gets to observe how Dad handles various situations.
8. As a coach, don't be overbearing.
9. Realize that wrestling is a 50–50 proposition. Only one hand gets raised. Someone has to lose.
10. Try to take a step back and look at what your child is going through overall, and I don't mean wins and losses. You have to appreciate the hard work your child is putting in.

Jack Childs's Favorite Drill

Round-Robin Defense

This is a four-man drill. The number one wrestler is in the middle of the circle.

The number two wrestler continually shoots on the number one wrestler for 15 seconds. Number one does not allow number two to get to his legs or body at all by constantly moving within the circle and by jamming the man's hands and shoulders. The number three wrestler follows number two for 15 seconds. The number four wrestler follows number three for 15 seconds.

Then number two is in the center with three, four, and one.
Then number three is in the center with four, one, and two.
Finally, number four is in the center with one, two, and three.

The result is that the man in the center is there for 45 seconds constantly on defense and moving!

25

My Two Champions

John Irving, Writer and Former Prep School Coach

The following is an excerpt from John Irving's memoir, The Imaginary Girlfriend. *A great American novelist, Irving was a wrestler at Phillips Exeter Academy in New Hampshire and the University of Pittsburgh before he transferred to the University of New Hampshire. He coached his two older sons, Colin and Brendan, during their high school wrestling careers. His youngest son, Everett, is a skier and interested in opera. Irving was inducted into the Wrestling Hall of Fame in 1992. He won an Academy Award for his screenplay,* The Cider House Rules, *in 2000.*

I taught creative writing, at one place or another, for a total of 11 years; yet I continued to coach wrestling long after the publication of *The World According to Garp* freed me of the financial need for an outside job. I coached until 1989, when I was 47, not only because I preferred coaching to teaching but for a variety of other reasons; the foremost reason was the success of my two elder sons in the sport—they were better wrestlers (and better athletes) than I had been, and coaching them meant more to me than my own modest accomplishments as a competitor.

Colin, who wrestled at Northfield Mount Hermon, was a prep-school All-American at 152 pounds—at the annual Lehigh tournament in 1983. Colin also won the New England Class A title at 160 pounds in '83; ironically, he pinned a guy from Exeter in the finals. Colin was voted the Outstanding Wrestler in the Class A tournament, for which he received the Ted Seabrooke Memorial trophy. I would have been happier if Ted had been alive to see Colin win the championship. Ted had seen Colin wrestle only once, when Colin was just starting the sport.

"He's got much longer arms than *you* ever had," Coach Seabrooke told me. "You ought to show him a crossface-cradle." By the time Colin was a Class A Champion and an All-American, he was pinning half his opponents with a crossface-cradle.

At six feet two and a half, Colin was tall for a middleweight. I think that his college coach was well intentioned but mistaken to put Colin on a weight-lifting program in order to beef him up to the 177-pound class, and then to 190. Colin was not a natural light heavyweight; he was at his best as a *tall* middle-weight. Nowadays—Colin is 30 years old—he stays out of the weight room and rides a mountain bike; he's a very lean 175.

His younger brother Brendan was, like me, a lightweight; unlike me, Brendan was a *tall* lightweight—at five feet eleven and a half, Brendan is so thin that he looks like a six-footer. (I'm only five feet eight, "normal" for a lightweight.) Unremarkably, both Colin and Brendan grew up in wrestling rooms; rolling around on a mat was second nature to them—I remember that Brendan learned to walk on a wrestling mat. Unlike Colin, who didn't start competing as a wrestler before his prep-school years, Brendan had already won six junior-school New England tournaments before his prep-school career began. (Brendan won his first wrestling tournament at the

weight of 82½ pounds.) By the time Brendan was wrestling for Vermont Academy, the other wrestlers—and, especially, the other coaches—in the New England Class A league were watching him closely to see if he would live up to the reputation of being Colin Irving's little brother; this was a burden for Brendan, largely because his proneness to injury was unlike anything Colin had ever suffered.

Brendan placed third in the New England Class A tournament his sophomore year at Vermont Academy; it was a good finish to a bad season for him, because the tournament was only a month after he'd had knee surgery for torn cartilage—he'd missed most of the '87 season. In '88, he was seeded second in the Class A tournament; he'd had an undefeated dual-meet season, excepting two losses to injury-default. Then, in the semifinals of the tournament, he reinjured the knee and was pinned by a boy he'd pinned earlier in the season; the injury forced him to drop out of the Class A's—and he reinjured the same knee at the Navy wrestling camp in Annapolis that summer. He spent the rest of the summer and the fall in physical therapy.

Colin lost a close match in the Class A finals his junior year—to a boy he'd beaten easily in the dual-meet season. Colin didn't win the New England Class A title until his senior year. Brendan's senior year began badly. A separated shoulder and a torn rotator-cuff tendon eliminated him from a Christmas tournament. Brendan was the 1989 team captain at Vermont Academy, but he would spend the heart of the season on the bench. When his shoulder healed, he was back in the lineup for three matches; he won all three—then he sat out another three weeks with mononucleosis. (Then he knocked out a front tooth.)

The week before the New England Class A's, Brendan was wrestling at St. Paul's when the St. Paul's wrestler, who was losing at the time and repeatedly being put in a crossface-cradle, bent back two of Brendan's fingers on his right hand and broke them at the big knuckle joints. Under the finger bending rule (all four or none), Brendan won the match, despite having to default with the injury. But the damage had been done: the fingers wouldn't heal by the time of the tournament—Brendan would wrestle at the Class A's with two broken fingers.

To add insult to injury, the mother of the St. Paul's wrestler objected to the referee's decision to award the match to Brendan because of her son's illegal hold; when a wrestler is injured by an ille-

gal hold, and cannot continue to wrestle, he wins. But the St. Paul's mother declared that Brendan had been injured prior to the match; she'd seen a Band-Aid on one of his fingers—one of the now broken fingers. (Brendan had skinned a knuckle while scraping the ice off his car's windshield that morning, on his way to weigh-in.) I had to restrain myself from sending the St. Paul's mother a videocassette of the match. The St. Paul's wrestler not only clearly broke Brendan's fingers; with his other hand, Brendan was pointing to his bent fingers—to draw the referee's attention to the foul—when the two fingers broke. The ref had made the right call, but he should have spotted the injury-in-progress—he could have prevented it.

Given the accumulation of Brendan's injuries, and his small number of matches in the '89 season, the seeding committee at the New England Class A tournament was entirely justified in seeding Brendan no higher than fifth in the 135-pound weight class; there were seven other wrestlers in the weight class with winning records. As his coach—I was an assistant coach at Vermont Academy for one year and the head coach for Brendan's last two seasons—I had contemplated moving Brendan up to the 140-pound class. In previous seasons, Brendan had pinned the two best wrestlers who would be the finalists in that weight class; in the 1989 Class A's, 140 was a weaker weight than 135. But Brendan, who was always admirably stubborn—even as a small child—insisted that 135 was *his* weight class; he didn't want to move up. (No wrestler wants to move up a weight class.)

The New England Class A tournament was at Exeter that year—in the new gym, where I'd never wrestled. (I have no idea what the pit is used for now.) I had a good team at little Vermont Academy in '89. In the Class A team standings, we would finish third—behind Deerfield and Exeter, two much bigger schools. I would send three Vermont Academy wrestlers to the finals, and two of them would win—Brendan was one of Vermont's two champions. He pinned the number-four seed from Northfield Mount Hermon in the quarterfinals, he pinned the number-one seed from Hyde in the semifinals and he pinned the number-two seed from Worcester in the finals; he stuck his broken fingers, which were rebroken in the semifinals, in a bucket of ice in between the rounds.

Tom Williams, who would die of cancer in three years, came to the tournament. Colin was there. My wife, Janet, was there; for two

years, she'd not missed a match of Brendan's—and she'd taken what seemed, at the time, to be an excessive number of photographs. (As time passes, I'm grateful for every picture.) My mother had come up from Florida to see the tournament. And my old Exeter teammate, Charles C. ("Brute") Krulak—*General* Krulak—had come to see Brendan, too. Chuck had seen Brendan win the Lakes Region tournament (now known as the Northern New England tournament) the previous year; he'd promised Brendan that he would come to see him wrestle in the New England Class A's—but only if Brendan would promise to win the tournament. Brendan had promised, and Brendan had done it. (To be truthful, I'd always known he *could*. But he'd been so banged-up, I didn't think he *would*.)

I had spent so many hours of my life at wrestling tournaments, and so many more hours in wrestling rooms. After Exeter and Pittsburgh and Iowa and Windham, there were the hours in the wrestling room at Amherst College and at the Buckingham Browne & Nichols School—and at Harvard, at the New York Athletic Club, at Northfield Mount Hermon, and at Vermont Academy, too. It was the perfect closure . . . that it should end at Exeter, where it began. I knew I would be a visitor to the occasional wrestling room, and that I would still put on the shoes—if only to roll around on the mat with Colin or Brendan, or with any other old ex-wrestler of my generation—but my life in wrestling effectively ended there.

I put my Vermont Academy wrestlers on the team bus with my co-coach, Mike Kennelly, and I asked Mike and the team to forgive me for not riding on the bus with them one last time. I wanted to ride back to Vermont in Colin's car, with Colin and Brendan. On the long drive home (we were still somewhere in New Hampshire), Colin picked up a speeding ticket—shortly after delivering a lecture to Brendan and me about the infallibility of his new radar-detection system. But we could laugh about the ticket. Brendan, like his older brother before him, had won the New England Class A title. It was the happiest night of my life.

26
Wrestling with Politics

James Jordan, Ohio Senator

Ohio State Senator Jim Jordan was in the early throes of orchestrating his re-election campaign for the Fourth District congressional seat in November of 2005. Jordan was going about things with his usual drive, focus, intensity, and determination, using the work ethic he developed throughout his successful wrestling career to help boost his life in politics. A great defender of traditional conservative values, he is passionate about all issues that relate to families.

"It's sort of interesting. I ran for office for State Representative for the first time in 1994. I was definitely not supposed to win. I had never been in politics before. I was coaching wrestling, and I was living in a Republican part of Ohio. No

Jim Jordan, senator from Ohio, uses the skills he learned in wrestling to boost his political campaign.
(Photo courtesy of Jim Jordan campaign headquarters.)

one thought I could win. I got busy, applied the same work ethic that I used in wrestling, and out-hustled the opponent," Jordan explained.

Not only did Jordan out-hustle his opponent in that race, but he won big as he took every county. Then in 2000 Jordan decided to run for Ohio's State Senate. Ohio is a seven-county district so he had four new counties to claim.

"That senate primary was the biggest in the history of Ohio. My opponent had money and everyone from the state endorsed him. My campaign was backed by wrestlers and good pro-family voters. I knocked on thousands of doors. In the end, I won big and I attribute it all to wrestling," he said.

The greatest thing that Jordan holds on to from his days as a wrestler is self-discipline. His high school coach was a tough teacher and a tough coach, and Jordan learned a lot of lessons about self-discipline.

"Discipline is about doing the things you may not want to do. Discipline is doing it the coach's way, not your own way. You have to train right and lift right and do it consistently," he said.

Jordan explained that his father encouraged him to try wrestling because at 5'7", the NFL didn't look like a possibility. Once he started with wrestling, he was hooked. His biggest win came during his freshman year when he won the state tournament.

"I won because I didn't know that freshmen weren't supposed to win state tournaments," he said. "I learned early that if you set goals and work hard, then good things can happen."

Jordan was a four-time Ohio State champion with a career record of 150-1. He went on to the University of Wisconsin where he was a two-time NCAA champion and a two-time Big 10 champion. Later he was an assistant coach at Ohio State from 1987–95.

Interestingly, Ben, Jordan's son, is following in his father's footsteps, having won the high school state tournament at 119 pounds in 2005 as a freshman. At the start of the season he didn't make the starting varsity spot, then he earned it, and then he lost it in a wrestle-off again. After losing that last wrestle-off, he refocused, won the starting spot back again, and moved on to win the league, the section, the district, and the state tournament.

"That's a tough weight class, but he did it. His freshman year was a storybook year. The three days at the state tournament were fun. I think it was even more special because I got to see my son do it. The skill level of school boy wrestlers these days is amazing," the elder Jordan said.

Jordan thinks it's important for young athletes to get involved in wrestling because of the lessons that can be learned from the sport.

"I think involvement in sports is good in general. That's where you can learn discipline and toughness. Out of all the sports, though, wrestling is so intense. There's just something about it because it is so physical. Wrestling puts you in situations that require great focus and intensity, and that carries over into everything you do in life. I think that the type of discipline you learn from wrestling is what more kids in this country need," he said.

27

He Stands Alone

Coach Jack Spates, University of Oklahoma

Coach Jack Spates became the 12th head wrestling coach at the University of Oklahoma in 1993. Spates was named the 2006 NWCA (National Wrestling Coaches Association) Coach of the Year after the Sooners finished in third place at the NCAA finals. That same year he was named the Co-Big 12 Coach of the Year, which marked the third time he received the honor.

Spates has an overall career coaching record of 307-90-8. Prior to Oklahoma, he coached at Cornell from 1988–93.

Spates, who has four children, is also a songwriter who has written ballads for all five of his national champions. The following is one of the ballads that he wrote for John Kading, his 1997 champion.

He Stands Alone

A young boy lies awake at night wishing on a star,
Thinking 'bout the road of life he'd like to travel far.
While other boys think games and toys,
As they lay down for the night,
He's got a dream of glory set firmly in his sight,
And he's not afraid to stand alone,
And he's not afraid to walk alone.

He came upon an ancient art from the days of old,
It was the sport of warriors of the fearless and the bold.
He knew he'd never settle to stand among the rest,
He'd pay the price of glory. He would be the best,
For he's not afraid to stand alone,
And he's not afraid to walk alone.

He'd run the lonely hours of the morning,
He'd work into the dark of night,
He never let his dreams of glory from his sight.

He traveled to the land of lakes,
And there for all to see,
He stood before the thousands
To meet his destiny.
Two men fought in fury,
And when it was all done,
He rose above his vanquished foe . . .
Then there was just one.
For he's not afraid to stand alone,
And he's not afraid to walk alone,
And now he stands . . . all alone.

28
Drills

- Knock-Out Drill
- Down Block Drill
- High Crotch Head Block Spin Drill
- Squaring Hips Drill
- Single Leg Head Block Spin Drill
- Monkey Grip Go Behind Drill
- Snap a Wrist to an Underhook Throw-By Drill
- Post Triceps Drill
- Knee Slide Drill
- Bull Fight Drill
- Hip Heist Drill
- Stand-Up Mat Return Drill
- Spiral Ride Claw Drill

Knock-Out Drill

The knock-out drill helps to develop the skills needed to nullify an opponent's attack and break his position. This drill practices using heavy hips.

Starting in a stance, the wrestler visualizes an attack on one leg and drops that same leg back. He drops his hip from that same leg to the mat and circles away from the hip that is down.

Left: Wrestler gets in his stance and visualizes a leg attack.
Above: He drops his leg back and drops to his knee.

He pushes up to his knee.

He quickly moves to a tri-pod position.

He circles away from the hip that was down.

Down Block Drill

The down block drill is used to practice protecting the leg when a wrestler is on his feet. It is important to maintain good stance position and lead with the head throughout this drill.

Wrestler starts from his stance.

From his stance level motion he shifts his weight to his outside foot and down blocks with his arm.

Drills

He drops his head and his hand hits the mat.

He pulls his leg back.

High Crotch Head Block Spin Drill

The head block spin drill teaches a wrestler to react to a high crotch attack by blocking with his head and spinning behind the opponent.

Here's a look from both sides of a head block by the wrestler in black to counter his opponent's high-crotch attack.

Drills

The wrestler in black puts his hand on his opponent's elbow and keeps his head in blocking position.

The wrestler in black does an elbow pass and forces his opponent's arm to the mat.

The offensive wrestler pulls his leg back and spins behind.

Squaring Hips Drill

The squaring hips drill helps wrestlers learn to respond to a single leg attack with heavy hips.

The wrestler in black shoots in a single leg and pulls his own leg back while his head is pushed to the mat.

He circles behind to attack both knees.

He circles to the opposite side of the single leg and attacks the near knee.

He slides down to a single leg, isolates the knee, and puts his head in the hole.

The wrestler in white squares with heavy hips over his opponent's head.

He breaks his opponent down to the mat.

Single Leg Head Block Spin Drill

The single leg head block spin drill teaches a wrestler how to counter a single leg attack. When an opponent shoots a single leg, this drill teaches a wrestler to drop his head into his opponent's chin, pull the leg back, push his arm by and spin behind him.

The wrestler in white changes his level and attacks on a single leg. The wrestler in black matches his stance.

The wrestler in black blocks with his head in his opponent's shoulder and turns his head into his chin. At the same time he pulls back the leg that is being attacked.

The wrestler in black spins behind his opponent.

Then he follows with a complete spin to the opposite side.

Monkey Grip Go Behind Drill

This is another drill that focuses on snapping an opponent down to the mat to set up a takedown.

The wrestler in white applies pressure to the shoulders. The wrestler in black snaps his wrists.

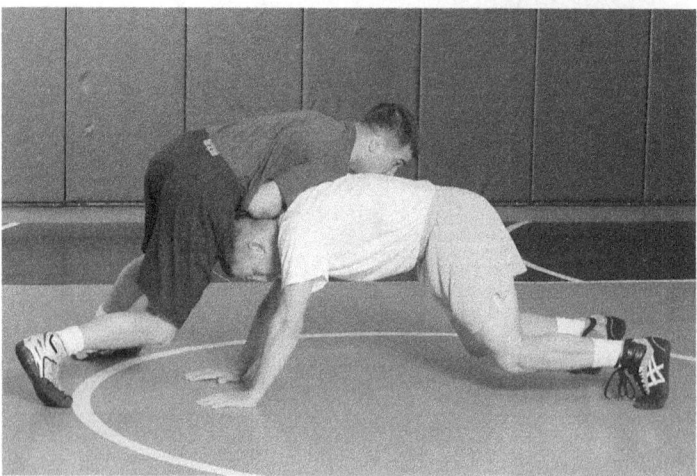

The wrestler in black crashes with his shoulder and he doubles up with his hands on his opponent's nearside arm. While the wrestler in black attempts to spin on the nearside, the wrestler in white counters from the bottom by spinning to face off.

The wrestler in black counters by pulling on triceps in a monkey grip.

The wrestler in black circles to a corner.

Monkey Grip Go Behind Drill, continued

He snaps his opponent to his hands.

He arm blocks and spins to the opposite side.

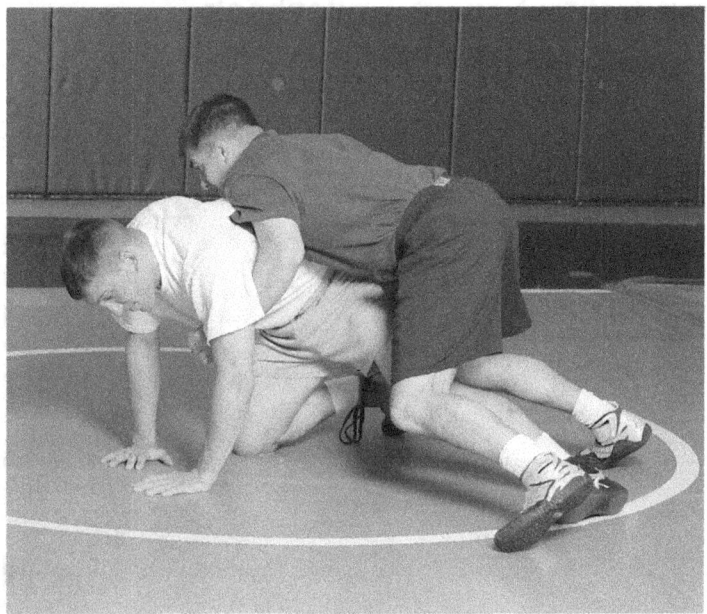

He spins behind, drives forward, and breaks his opponent down.

Snap a Wrist to an Underhook Throw-By Drill

This drill teaches a wrestler to snap a wrist and move to an underhook throw-by.

The wrestler in white puts pressure on shoulders.

The wrestler in black pulls his shoulder back and snaps wrist.

He uses the arm that snapped the wrist to feed to an underhook.

He secures the underhook and keeps his elbow tight to the ribs.

Snap a Wrist to an Underhook Throw-By Drill, continued

He starts a windmill motion . . .

. . .

He pancakes his arm through until the opponent hits the mat.

He finishes with a spin behind.

Post Triceps Drill

Post drills help wrestlers to open space and prevent an opponent from down blocking. When working on posting, it is important to maintain a good stance.

The wrestler in white puts pressure on shoulders.

The opponent lowers his level, doubles his hands on his triceps and forces the arms up.

He steps into a high-crotch penetration.

Drills 191

He slides his head, attacks the far knee while maintaining shoulder-knee alignment.

This is a look at the opposite side where the far knee is attacked.

Post Triceps Drill, continued

He swivels his hips around the corner and drives on a double.

He drives his opponent with a double leg finish.

Knee Slide Drill

This knee slide drill practices the penetration step and it continues with one partner sprawling and one re-shooting.

The wrestler in white penetrates to a high crotch.

The opponent sprawls back.

Knee Slide Drill, continued

The wrestler in white drives off his back leg, shoots his knee.

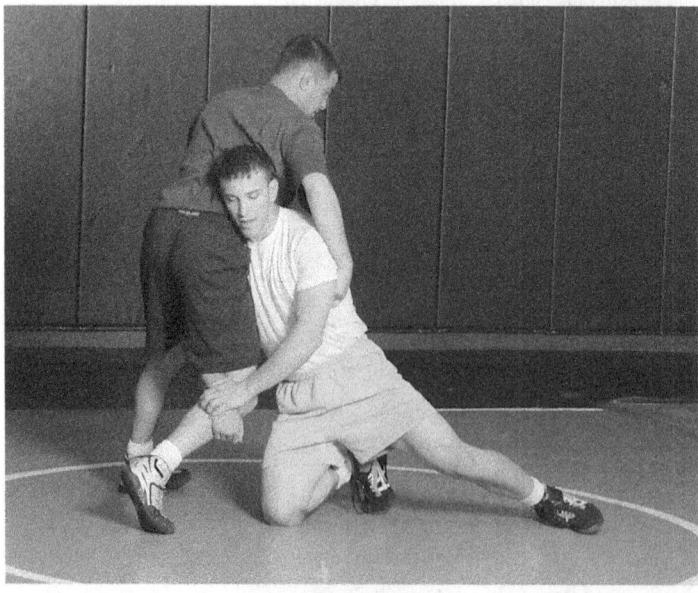

He secures a leg while maintaining shoulder-knee alignment.

Bull Fight Drill

The bull fight drill works on steering the opponent, stepping to a corner and creating an angle.

The wrestler in black hits an inside tie, while his other hand posts the shoulder.

The hand posting the shoulder slides into a collar tie-up.

Bull Fight Drill, continued

He uses his body weight to snap and draw the leg back.

He switches the inside tie to an elbow pass down and across his opponent's body while releasing the pressure on the head. The opponent automatically stands up.

He quickly takes advantage of white being out of position by setting up a shot to the opposite side.

He repeats with an elbow pass across the body.

Bull Fight Drill, continued

He hits a penetration step to a high crotch.

Hip Heist Drill

The hip heist drill teaches movement from scramble situations.

Wrestler balances himself on his hands and feet to start.

He hits a cross-understep and swivels hips.

Hip Heist Drill, continued

He swivels with his hips while keeping his butt from hitting the mat.

He alternates his feet while swiveling his hips with a cross understep.

Drills  201

Stand-Up Mat Return Drill

This drill has one wrestler working on stand-ups while the other works on mat returns.

From the referee's position, the bottom wrestler hits a standup. He needs to maintain a straight back with his elbows in as he comes to his feet.

The wrestler in black posts a leg.

The wrestler in white follows his opponent.

Stand-Up Mat Return Drill, continued

He locks his hands around his opponent's torso and steps a corner.

He steps his hips in and pops up his opponent.

He returns his opponent to the mat while trying to gain wrist control.

Spiral Ride Claw Drill

The goal in using a spiral ride is to get your opponent flat on the mat by putting a lot of weight on his upper body and driving forward in a circular motion.

Starting from the referee's position, the wrestler in black slides his front arm to a claw and his tight-waist arm moves to a pocket ride.

The wrestler in black pinches his elbows tight and gets up on his toes.

He circles toward his opponent's head while the pocket ride arm pulls the hip to the mat.

Spiral Ride Claw Drill, continued

The opponent hits the mat.

The wrestler in black switches sides to trap the hip.

He shoots the high hand to a claw and drives his opponent to his back.

Index

A

Academics, 6, 35–36, 42, 70
Accountability, personal, 72
Adams, Carl, 77, 81–87
Andersson, Frank, 136
Anspach, Rob, 70, 71, 72, 73
Anticipation, 86
Armstrong, Jack, 60
Assistant coaches, 67–73

B

Bahr, Dale, 77
Bartelma, David, 90, 91
Bevilacqua, Al, 153, 154
Bonfiglio, Ryan, 41–42
Borlaug, Dr. Norman, 89–93
Borrelli, Jason, 154
Borrelli, Tom, 127–29, 154, 155
Brady, Tom, 44
Brands, Nelson, 34
Brands, Terry, 31–36, 151–52
Brands, Tom, 96–98, 151
Buckley, Brendan, 37, 38, 40, 41
Bull fight drill, 195–98
Bush, George W., 11, 55

C

Camp of Champs, 77, 80
Carroll, Paul, 107

Childs, Jack, 154, 155–58
Churella, Josh, 148
Churella, Mark, Jr., 148, 149
Churella, Mark, Sr., 148–51
Churella, Ryan, 148, 149
Coaching ethics, 31–36
Criticism, constructive, 6, 97–98

D

Determination, 101
Dillon, Corey, 44
Disability, Best Athlete with a, 23–29
Donovan, Tim, 107, 108, 109, 111–15
Down block drill, 174–75
Drills, wrestling
   bull fight drill, 195–98
   down block drill, 174–75
   easy-in, hard-out, 129
   hard drilling, 53
   high crotch head block spin drill, 176–77
   hip heist drill, 199–200
   knee slide drill, 193–94
   knock-out drill, 172–73
   level change, 48
   monkey grip go behind drill, 182–85
   penetration drill, 120
   post triceps drill, 190–92

Index

round-robin defense, 158
single leg head block spin drill, 180–81
situations, 126
snap a wrist to an underhook throw-by drill, 186–89
spiral ride claw drill, 203–4
squaring hips drill, 178–79
stand-up mat return drill, 201–2

E

Easy-in, hard-out, 129
Esposito, Zach, 152
Ethics, coaching, 31–36

F

Fathers, advice from, 147–58
Favorite drills
    easy-in, hard-out, 129
    hard drilling, 53
    level change, 48
    penetration drill, 120
    round-robin defense, 158
    situations, 126
Football and wrestling, 43–48
Ford, Gerald, 11
Fraser, Steve, 135–39

G

Gable, Dan, 3, 15–22, 45, 77, 78, 79, 103
Gable principle, 96
Gillis, Shawn, 107
Grind matches, 139

H

Hard drilling, 53
Harkness, John, 152
Harvard wrestling team
    head coach, 37, 38, 39–40, 41
    mission statement, 40–41
Hastert, Dennis, 55–60
Hastert, Ethan, 60
Hastert, Jean, 60
Hastert, Joshua, 60
Heffernan, Jim, 67–70
Heinbaugh, Rich, 76
High crotch head block spin drill, 176–77
Hip heist drill, 199–200
Hobbies, 121–25
Hofstra's assistant coaches, 70–73

I

Injuries, guarding against, 83
Irving, Brendan, 159, 160–62, 163
Irving, Colin, 159, 160, 161, 162, 163
Irving, Everett, 159
Irving, Janet, 162
Irving, John, 159–63

J

Jantzen, Donald, 152
Jantzen, Jesse, 38–39, 40, 152, 153
Jean, Chuck, 77
Johnson, Mark, 67, 69
Jordan, Ben, 167
Jordan, James, 165–67
Journal, wrestling, 137–38

Index

K

Kading, John, 169–70
Kennelly, Mike, 163
Kerr, T. J., 44, 46, 47, 48, 125–27
King, Billie Jean, 62
Kline, Camryn, 145
Kline, Laura, 145
Kline, Sam, 141–46
Knee slide drill, 193–94
Knock-out drill, 172–73
Kraft, Art, 99, 100
Kraft, Ken, 99–103
Krulak, Charles C., 163

L

Lee, Reggie, 39
Level-changing drill, 48
Lincoln, Abraham, 59–60
Losing, learning from, 95–98

M

Martin, Dave, 77
Maynard, Anita, 24
Maynard, Kyle, 23–29
Maynard, Scott, 24
McLaughlin, Donny, 106
McLaughlin, Father John, 105–10, 112–14
McLaughlin, Gary, 106
McLaughlin, Keith, 106
Meltzer, Max, 39
Mental imagery, 84–85
Mental toughness, 135–39
Midlands Tournament, 80, 100, 101–3

Mission statement, Harvard wrestling team, 40–41
Mistakes, handling, 97–98
Monkey grip go behind drill, 182–85

N

Neal, Stephen, 43–48
New England Patriots, 43–48, 109–10
Nichols, Harold, 77
Nixon, Richard, 11
No Excuses, 26
No Excuses Principle, 24, 25
Nobel Peace Prize winner, 89–93
Number of wrestlers, 20
Nutrition, 6, 81, 82, 97

O

Off-season, 118–19
Ogunwole, Bode, 39
Olympic gold, 17, 75–80, 135–39
One-hour go practice, 122
Outdoor education classes, 125–27
Overtraining, 6–7
Owings, Larry, 16

P

Parents, advice from, 147–58
Peaking, 81–85
Penetration drill, 120
Perseverance, 12

Index

Peterson, Ben, 45–46, 75–80
Peterson, John, 77, 78, 79
Peterson, Mrs., 79
Peterson, Phil, 76
Petrov, Roussi, 79
Pickerill, Ken, 56, 57
Pierson, Joyce, 14
Politicians
    Ohio senator, 165–67
    Speaker of the House, 55–60
Posters, 52
Pritzlaff, Donny, 70, 71, 73
Promotion, program, 49–53

R

Ramos, Cliff, 25
Recovery time, 21, 83
Recruiting, 72–73, 85, 101
Referees, 131–34
Riggs, Bobby, 62
Robinson, J, 49–53
Round-robin defense, 158
Rules, team, 4–5
Rumsfeld, Donald, 9–14
Rumsfeld, George, 10
Ryan, Jake, 3
Ryan, Jordan, 3
Ryan, Lynette, 3
Ryan, Mackenzie, 3
Ryan, Teague, 3, 4
Ryan, Tom, 1–7, 70, 71, 72, 73

S

Sanderson, Cael, 24, 86
Saunders, Townsend, 63
Saunders, Tricia, 61–66
Seabrooke, Ted, 160
Seinfeld, Jerry, 153
Self-discipline, 120, 166, 167
Shumilin, Andrei, 45
Single leg head block spin drill, 180–81
Smith, Jason, 77
Snap a wrist to an underhook throw-by drill, 186–89
Spates, Jack, 169–70
Speaker of the House, 55–60
Speed, 85–87
Spiral ride claw drill, 203–4
Squaring hips drill, 178–79
Steiner, Terry, 63
Strakhov, Ennado, 79
Strobel, Greg, 47, 48, 121–25

T

Taylor, Chris, 77
Team rules, 4–5
Team unity, building
    family atmosphere for, 127–29
    gut-busting workouts for, 35
    hobbies for, 121–25
    wilderness adventures for, 125–27
30 × 30 practice, 122
Time management, 156
Timing, 86
Tips
    on handling mistakes, 98
    for parents, 155, 157
    on tournaments, 103

Tournament, running a, 101–3
Tragedy, overcoming, 111–15
Turner, John, 107, 110

U

U.S. Wrestling Officials Association, 132
University of Illinois, 67–70
University of Iowa, 17, 69, 95–98, 117–20

W

Weight management, 6, 83, 156
Weiss, Jay, 37, 38, 39–40, 41
Wilderness adventures, 125–27
Williams, Tom, 162
Women's wrestling, 61–66
Work ethic, 37
Wrestling drills
  bull fight drill, 195–98
  down block drill, 174–75
  easy-in, hard-out, 129
  hard drilling, 53
  high crotch head block spin drill, 176–77
  hip heist drill, 199–200
  knee slide drill, 193–94
  knock-out drill, 172–73
  level change, 48
  monkey grip go behind drill, 182–85
  penetration drill, 120
  post triceps drill, 190–92
  round-robin defense, 158
  single leg head block spin drill, 180–81
  situations, 126
  snap a wrist to an underhook throw-by drill, 186–89
  spiral ride claw drill, 203–4
  squaring hips drill, 178–79
  stand-up mat return drill, 201–2

Y

Year-round wrestling, 117–20

Z

Zalesky, Jim, 117–20
Zuaro, Dr. Vincent, 131–34

About the Authors

Tom Ryan became the head coach at Ohio State University in 2006. Ryan coached the Hofstra University wrestling team for 11 seasons and is a two-time New York State Coach of the Year. As a college wrestler, Ryan was a two-time NCAA Division I All-American and a member of the University of Iowa's national championship teams under Coach Dan Gable in 1991 and 1992. A two-time Big 10 Conference champion at Iowa, Ryan wrestled for two years at Iowa after transferring from Syracuse University, where he captured an Eastern Intercollegiate Wrestling Association (EIWA) championship in 1989.

Ryan is married to Lynette, and they live in Ohio with their children, Jordan, Jake, and Mackenzie.

Julie Sampson published *Beginning Wrestling*, her first book about wrestling, in 2000. She teamed up with Tom Ryan and photographer Bruce Curtis to produce the fundamental guide to the sport.

Sampson has had many articles published in *Newsday*, *New York Times*, and *American Cheerleader* magazine. She was the sports editor for Imprint Newspapers in West Hartford, Connecticut. Over the years, she has acquired a deep appreciation for wrestling.

Sampson is married to John, and they live on Long Island with their two children, Troy and Sheila.

www.ingramcontent.com/pod-product-compliance
Lightning Source LLC
Chambersburg PA
CBHW081834170426
43199CB00017B/2731